How to Help Your Child Become Drug Free

A Guide for Parents of Adolescents & Young Adults with Substance Abuse or Addiction

Jon Daily, LCSW, CADC II
Recovery Happens Counseling Services
7996 Old Winding Way #300
Fair Oaks, CA 95628
916-276-0626
www............com

by

David Gust, CADC II, NCAC II
Sheila Walker, CADC II
Jon Daily, LCSW, CADC II

Acknowledgments

We would like to thank the people who helped us with this book. First of all, thank you to our editor, Paula Gangitano. Her wonderful editing skills and insights are responsible for a finished product for which we are very grateful.

Thank you to Carol Gust, Ruthmary Gust, Mary Euretig and Jeff Henigan for their readings and feedback.

Thank you to Kelly Collins for his contribution.

We would also like thank Dan Marquez, our colleague who has been our support through this process.

About the Authors

David, Sheila and Jon have a combined 45 years of experience as drug and alcohol counselors in the greater Sacramento, California area. We specialize in working with adolescents and young adults in an outpatient private practice setting. We offer a structured program that was developed by David Gust in the early 1980's. In addition to counseling, we provide training for other counselors, present educational community seminars, and teach at various higher educational institutions. In addition, we have contributed to local newspaper articles, news reports and radio presentations regarding adolescent/young adult substance abuse issues.

To contact us:
Call: (916) 966-4523

Our address is:
7996 Old Winding Way, Suite #300
Fair Oaks, CA 95628

Our website:
newdirectionsprogram.com

David Gust's website:
davidgust.net

Jon Daily's website:
recoveryhappens.com

Contents

Chapter 1

A Look at the Problem

You suspect your child has been using drugs. Maybe you know this for sure. Maybe you are worried about a friend, student, neighbor or co-worker. Whichever the case, you are concerned and probably don't know what to do. This book will help educate you about drug problems and offer necessary support and guidance as you navigate through their challenges. We recommend that you study the information that is of immediate interest to you. Become familiar with the terminology defined in the text and used to discuss the matter of drugs. Just as other endeavors such as a new job, hobby, politics or pop culture come with particular jargon, so does the ongoing discussion of drug use. This book will explain how to get help for yourself or the individual for whom you are concerned. If you are confused by the changes you have observed in someone who you know is using drugs or alcohol, we will explain the likely reasons for those changes. This book is intended to be a companion and teacher until you can get to the counselor's office or to a twelve-step meeting. We hope it will continue to serve as a reference and a tool to increase your understanding of the problem. We want to provide you with an accurate depiction of drug abuse and we want to dispel its accompanying myths. **The problem of adolescent drug use is not one that will resolve itself by ignoring it or pretending it does not exist.** It is to everyone's advantage to take immediate action in order to mitigate a drug problem.

In the following chapters, we will acquaint you with stages of drug use and the particularly rapid progression of those stages for adolescents. We will explain how parents, family members and friends, as well as others within the community unknowingly contribute to an adolescent's drug problem. Most importantly, we will supply you with a plan to deal with the problem and specific tools to reinforce that plan. We will clarify your role and responsibilities in the process and stress the importance of availing yourself of the many resources that exist to help you.

At the present time you may feel isolated. As soon as you begin to learn about drug abuse, you will realize that you do not have to deal with this problem alone. Drug use is common and exists in most every public and private school from the upper primary grades through college. It is a problem that crosses all social and economic lines and can be devastating to individuals, their families and society in general. Fear that the problem cannot be resolved keeps many people from seeking help. Ignorance about the problem actually perpetuates it. There *are* definite strategies that you can employ to arrest a drug problem. It is a problem that remains powerful, in part, because of the secrecy it demands. As families learn to deal openly with drug problems, they will be able to take steps to restore the peace and sanity they once had.

Peace and sanity? Do those aspects of life seem to have slipped away? Are they gone altogether? Are you fighting frequently with your spouse about your child's behavior or constantly second-guessing the child who you could formerly count on without fail? When your adolescent displays new behavior, introduces new friends, expresses new thoughts and attitudes and *you* are simultaneously feeling a sustained discomfort, you need to pay attention to your personal radar screen. It is difficult to determine whether all this newness is about hormones and healthy rebellion or if there is something more serious going on.

With the presence of drug use, the balance of a family's dynamics is interrupted. A foremost requirement of an individual's involvement with drugs is that he or she must keep his or her use secret. Some of the reasons for this are obvious. It is an illegal activity and one to which parents, schools, employers and society strongly object. In addition to a host of negative repercussions, including the dangers to health and safety, the usage itself is the catalyst for the erosion of trust in interpersonal relationships. People who are chemically dependent will lie to protect their ability and opportunities to use drugs.

As an individual's involvement increases, the need to protect the secrecy of drug use becomes more vehement. Less and less, your adolescent participates in school and family affairs. His ready excuses for missed appointments, failing grades, broken curfews or blood-shot eyes, while sounding plausible, simply lack credibility. After unsatisfactory explanations and breaches in the family's rules or traditions, parents start to doubt their child. Through his actions or attitudes, the youngster somehow manages to become the near-exclusive focus of the family, but not for the right reasons! Trust between the child and his parents or between other family members continues to degrade; negative behaviors tend to escalate and become repetitive and emotions often soar out of control. The characterization of the family may evolve to one of tension and behavioral extremes.

The child who becomes involved in drugs does not envision the destructive nature of his use. As you will see, the problem begins quite innocently and usually without fanfare. Notwithstanding the critical aspects of the child's health and safety, the damage caused by the erosion of trust between the child and his parents is the most formidable challenge at hand. Methods to meet this challenge do exist. Those who are seeking a quick resolve will be disappointed. Those who are eager to understand this challenge and whose motivation is a strong desire for change will stand the greatest chance for success. Anyone can accept this challenge. Please embrace the chapters that follow and consider the details, the examples and the rationale that we provide. We want the best possible outcome for you and your family.

Chapter 2

The Stages of Drug Use and
Their Rapid Progression

An adolescent may become dependent on chemicals early in his use of drugs. If he has a genetic predisposition to chemical dependency, he might experience symptoms immediately. Due to the insidious nature of drug abuse, your child may develop an addiction before you are even aware that he has been using drugs. Several factors contribute to the rapid progression of drug use in adolescents. In this regard, it will be helpful to examine the differences in drug usage between adolescents and adults.

Keep in mind that for adolescent drug users, drug use itself may be their single social event or recreation, the purpose of which is intoxication. Adult drinking, however, is generally only a part of a social event. For example, an adult may drink to toast to a newly married couple at a wedding and that toast will conclude any further alcohol consumption. The remainder of his time might be spent visiting with others, eating, listening to music or dancing. Although, as adults we may continue to hone our social skills and learn to adapt to different settings or situations, we have also had the benefit of and experience to develop socially. Childhood and adolescence constitute the time when practicing social skills begins. Learning to socialize and gain acceptance from their peers is crucial to adolescents. Most children expend a great deal of energy towards this end and the school day certainly affords them the opportunity to meet this challenge.

Understandably, parents tend to trust their children's school as a safe and reliable atmosphere. It is assumed that the student's focus is on academics and school-related activities. Unfortunately, school can be the *very* place to buy and sell drugs and to talk about how great it is to get high. Easy availability of drugs significantly contributes to the progression of drug use. Moreover, there is frequently tremendous peer pressure on campus that further serves to fuel the magnitude of the drug problem. Adults, by comparison, are more likely to be locked into very structured work settings and time constraints. They have inescapable responsibilities such as bill paying and maintaining a house. Generally, an adult's employment setting is separate from one's social pursuits. For high schoolers, work and play are integrated. Additionally, adults are more apt to use one drug exclusively while adolescents generally use a combination of drugs. This is referred to as "poly drug use." The use of different drugs increases the body's need for more drugs in order to achieve a desired physical or mental effect and a specific feeling of intoxication; this physiological condition is referred to as "tolerance."[1]

There is growing evidence to support the fact that an individual's genetic makeup, as well as his family background, may predispose him to chemical dependency, drug addiction and alcoholism. We recommend reading, *Uppers, Downers, All Arounders*, by Darryl S. Inaba and William E. Cohen for clarification on this most important subject. Keeping in mind the previously stated factors that have the ability to accelerate the progression of drug use, we will now illustrate and explain a model of the stages of drug use progression.

Joseph, an easily distracted hyperactive adolescent, was almost six months sober when he walked through the office door wearing a shirt depicting his favorite music group. His signature baseball cap was on backwards and he sported his usual baggy jeans. Plopping down on to the couch, he appeared contemplative. For two minutes, Joseph sat silently and reflected on his experience. He had never been quiet or still while in his counselor's office. He looked up suddenly! His face revealed an expression of enlightenment. His recollection of the following story demonstrates that he was beginning to put his drug use into perspective. With the tone of his voice sounding simultaneously like a statement and a question, he offered the following account:

"I think I can see what happened to me now.... I never wanted to use drugs. I remember having heard repeatedly from my parents and teachers that drugs were dangerous. I guess as I watched other kids use drugs I felt like I was supposed to use drugs too. I was around other kids who were using drugs and it didn't seem to be a problem for them. I would 'chill out' and watch them laughing and having fun while they got 'wasted.' I sat there feeling like I was missing out. I asked them what it was like. They all said it was 'cool' and that I should 'get high' just to try it. Then one time we hung out together, I decided to take a 'hit' from the 'joint' that they were smoking. *That was the first time I got high and that was when my*

7

addiction started. I remember laughing with the rest of them and, before I knew it, I asked them to pass me some more 'pot'. In an instant, I was one of them. It did not seem like a problem for me at the time. Shoot! As time went on I even made lots of new friends and I was invited to all kinds of parties. The next thing I knew I got 'wasted' every weekend and I was only 'chillin out' with drug users. Damn! I started smoking pot before and after school. I pulled away from my family, (emotionally) and I lied to them to get more money to buy pot. Man! My life really went down hill fast from there ...."

You will notice that the young man who shared his history of drug use spent a considerable amount of time observing and assessing other people doing drugs before ever smoking marijuana himself. This period of observation and consideration is referred to as the stage of *Contemplation.* **It is the point at which your child is deciding whether to use drugs.** It allows your child, who formerly was not around drugs and drug-using people, to find himself in an environment in which he is able to observe drug-using peers. Your child is watching his peers use alcohol or other drugs to see if it appears safe. He is watching his peers share drugs with each other, listening to them talking about the high they have experienced and realizing that they are relating to each other differently than he is relating to them because he is not yet using. In short, your child is intimately observing the "drug culture."

While that term is perhaps not as prevalent today, in the 1960's the *drug culture* referred to a social system in which all individuals, both male and female, shared a certain amount of equality. For instance, participants used a common language, wore similar attire and purported similar attitudes and political affiliations, in addition to sharing the key experience of intoxication. It was almost fraternity-like in that its members felt a loyalty and responsibility to the group and its values. Currently, drug culture is an abstract concept and may be too limiting to describe that part of today's adolescent population using drugs. Commercialism has dramatically influenced its tone and scope as evidenced by mass production of t-shirts, posters, videos and music. Even though today's drug culture may be difficult to define, we still agree that it is within a social environment where there are drug-using adolescents that your child can gain ready acceptance. It can afford your child the opportunity to weigh what it would be like to be part of a group, which condones using drugs. Your child can freely inquire about what it is like to use a particular drug. As your child becomes more comfortable around his drug-using peers and begins to rationalize drug use, he will move closer to his own usage.

Moving to actual intoxication occurs when your child starts to pass beers or joints to others in the room, meanwhile abstaining from his own personal use. Your child smells the beer when he passes it to another, smells the aroma of the burning marijuana as he passes a joint or pipe to a friend. A teen might begin to spend more time with drug users asking questions about intoxication, handling and smelling the drugs and wanting to fit into the non-judgmental, accepting drug culture. He contemplates drug use until he has convinced himself that trying drugs is okay.

As your child becomes more comfortable with the people who are using, it is likely that he will get closer to experiencing intoxication. He will not only smell the marijuana and alcohol, but also taste it, taking sips of his friends' beers or inhaling marijuana smoke as his drug-using friends exhale it. Contemplation, then, occurs as your child explores what it would be like to use drugs, but there is no chemical use.

After your child contemplates using drugs, the scene has been set for her to progress to stage two, that of *Experimentation*. During adolescence one seeks to discover his or her own identity through a process of examination and experimentation with new ideas, beliefs, values and behavior. Recalling our own teen years, we might remember painful struggles marked with extraordinary pressure from parents and peers. While this is naturally a difficult time for many adolescents, it may be coupled with the beginning of drug use. The usual phone call to our office is from a parent trying to determine the degree to which his child is involved in drug activity. The call is prefaced by the parent's concern that his child is *experimenting* with drugs. When we ask how long the parent has suspected his child has been using drugs, the answer might indicate about a year's time. Unfortunately, that parent's response indicates involvement well beyond experimentation. **Experimentation is a one-time event. Once your child has experienced intoxication, the experiment is complete.** After experiencing intoxication for the first time, an adolescent then determines whether he likes the effects of the drug. He will then make a decision whether to try or not to try the drug again based on that assessment.

If he continues to use drugs beyond this one-time event, he has progressed to stage three of drug use, *Misuse*. In this stage, chemical use is infrequent. Nevertheless, **misuse of chemicals is unhealthy and irresponsible behavior.** A child might use drugs on specified, celebratory occasions such as, New Year's Eve, Halloween, prom night, graduation, homecoming or at other events. The purpose of her use is to experience intoxication. At this point in the process, she has not yet developed a significant relationship with chemicals. Now, for the first time, she might begin to experience negative consequences due to her chemical use. Friends may tease her, she may experience hangovers, minor injuries or she may communicate less openly with you and other family members. While these consequences seem relatively mild, the reality is that even a first intoxication constitutes extremely high-risk behavior. It leaves an individual vulnerable to serious or even catastrophic car accident, physical injury, rape or overdose. It is important to note that many of the adolescents with whom we have worked have skipped this stage altogether and progressed immediately to substance abuse or drug addiction.

The fourth stage in the progression of drug use is termed *Substance Abuse*. At this time your child will develop a regular schedule of using. This schedule might include the weekends or the day he receives his allowance. We often hear substance abusers say that, "weekends are made for partying." Your child's frequent, scheduled use occurs because he has established an ongoing relationship with chemicals. He has started to trust chemicals because they relieve stress, anxiety, depression, anger, loneliness and the one feeling we hear about most often from adolescents, boredom. He realizes that chemicals are always available to him to alleviate a particular, uncomfortable feeling, even though he does not recognize his drug use as being related to his feelings. In the beginning of treatment for substance abuse and addiction, most adolescents will deny that their drug use is related to their feelings. However, chemicals can reliably change your child's moods and feelings.2/

As a teenager considers the normal questions that accompany adolescence, those that include issues of social and personal acceptance and rejection, sexuality and appearance, not only does he not always have adequate answers to his questions or someone in whom he can confide, he may also be desperate to rid himself of feelings that are unfamiliar or unpleasant. If drugs have made him feel better about himself or social conditions, then he might opt for relying on the use of drugs. It is also the good times and euphoria that motivate your child to continue his relationship with drugs. Your child experiences pleasure from drug use that, to him or her, far exceeds the pleasure provided by bicycle riding and playing video games. One of the things we tell our clients when we are helping them to see the consequences of their drug use, is that we will never discount their good times. We know they had fun using drugs or else they wouldn't have continued to use them. They continue to use in large part due to a key operative that perpetuates drug use: **Denial.**

Denial contributes to the continued use of drugs. We will mention here that denial is not to be confused with dishonesty. Denial is a psychological device that prevents your child from recognizing the negative activities and consequences surrounding his drug use. Dishonesty, however, involves an individual's deliberate, intentional act to manipulate a situation or its outcome. The word, "con", is a term used frequently within the specialty of drug-abuse counseling that refers to such dishonesty. As an adolescent begins to lose the connection between chemical use and undesirable consequences, he might experience trouble at home, with the law, friends, teachers or other authorities. This may include disciplinary actions such as the adolescent being grounded at home or suspended from school. *Substance abuse* **means using chemicals despite having experienced negative consequences.** When the connection between drug use and its consequences has become more and more *unclear* for your child, it has probably become more and more *clear* to you and the other concerned people in his life. Unfortunately, some parents and professionals buy the notion that all adolescents use drugs. This misinformation only contributes to the denial process and leads to further enabling of drug use. Denial, also, prevents the adolescent from feeling the accompanying guilt and anxiety surrounding his drug use. If your child were to perceive the effects of his use accurately, he would realize the necessity for quitting. Additionally, denial reinforces his perspective that all teens use drugs. Of course, this is not true.

Prior to a discussion about the stage of *Addiction,* a few general comments are in order. Not all drug users progress to chemical dependency, drug addiction or alcoholism. However, we regard any point during the progression as a drug problem. If your child is addicted to drugs, remember that he is addicted to intoxication, *not* to a particular drug. He might tell you that he is addicted to marijuana and then quit marijuana only to replace its use with alcohol. This is called "cross-addiction." Adolescents who are addicted to one drug are predisposed to cross-addiction. Some people, although rare in adolescents, will have physical addiction to a particular drug. In this case, a person has to keep using the drug to avoid the physically painful and sometimes dangerous symptoms of withdrawal. The majority of adolescents who are chemically dependent do not have physical addiction. **Adolescents who are experiencing physical symptoms or withdrawal require immediate medical intervention, which may include hospitalization.**

As we discussed previously, dishonesty is not to be confused with denial. However, dishonesty *is* instrumental in the perpetuation of drug involvement and can be thought of as, "the currency of adolescent drug use." Your child might not yet have marketable skills to earn his own money to pay for drugs and he can't just come out in the open and tell you that he likes to wake up in the morning and smoke marijuana. He can't tell his teacher he is getting high before class and that it is really fun. He can't tell you that he really likes to be high when he is playing his video games because he knows you would disapprove. Honesty about drug use means the beginning of the end of drug use. Your child learned very quickly to be dishonest so that he could continue getting high.

Drug addiction, chemical dependency and alcoholism are terms used interchangeably to describe a disease exhibiting the following characteristics:

1) Preoccupation;

2) Loss of interest;

3) Tolerance;

4) Physical withdrawal;

5) Loss of control;

6) Using drugs despite social, psychological or physical consequences; and

7) Unsuccessful attempts to cut down or quit using.

Preoccupation means that your child is putting most of his energy into drug use. For instance, your child may spend time daydreaming about and looking forward to getting high at the party he will attend Friday night. In addition to lying and attempting to manipulate people or circumstances, he may also spend time drawing pictures of chemicals or paraphernalia on notebooks, shoes, etc. or write continuously about drugs as a topic in his school assignments. Moreover, his preoccupation is exhibited by wearing clothing, such as shirts, hats, necklaces and other articles that refer to chemicals or paraphernalia. If your child is wearing clothing decorated with a marijuana leaf, for example, it could be a sign of your child's preoccupation with drugs. You may have already found yourself questioning him about the drug pictures on his bedroom walls or apparel, and he may have tried to convince you that everyone has them. He might tell you that you need to "quit tripping." Kids without drug problems don't put those kinds of pictures on their walls.

Loss of interest, too, plays an integral part in the insidious disintegration of physical and emotional health that accompanies drug use progression. If the majority of one's energies are devoted to thinking about intoxication or the acquisition of drugs, it's logical that other interests will be tabled to accommodate the present, pressing desire or need for drugs. Your child may defend his loss of interests in friends, sports, music or other activities with a host of excuses that may seem quite rational but nevertheless, appeal to a parent's own denial regarding his child's deteriorating social involvement or decline in physical activities or hobbies.

Tolerance is another characteristic of addiction. As mentioned earlier, this simply means that your child needs increasingly larger amounts of a chemical to get a desired or predictable effect. Adolescents with drug problems develop tolerance very quickly and, as their relationship with chemicals grows stronger, so do their bodies' tolerance to the drug. The toxic insult of chemicals to their brains and bodies demands that they take in larger and larger amounts of the drug, not only to get the desired effect, but with usage over time, just to feel normal. Many clients tell us, "Yeah I used to get a good 'buzz' on two beers, but now it takes five or six to get that same feeling." This statement reflects the fact that their bodies have developed tolerance. Tolerance occurs rapidly for stimulant users.[3/] Examples of stimulants include methamphetamine (crank), ecstasy and cocaine. If your child is a stimulant user the amount of his chemical use can increase significantly in just a few months. Some adolescents who are addicted might experience **physical withdrawal.** There is no set time for this occurrence. Withdrawal is the body's way of saying, "Now that you have made me sick, I want more chemicals to feel normal. I *need* chemicals to avoid withdrawal symptoms." The general symptoms of withdrawal can include cravings for the drug, anxiety, restlessness, and sleep problems. In more severe cases of withdrawal, the user will experience disorientation to space and time, hallucinations such as seeing fleas on the skin, hearing dogs barking or experiencing profuse sweating or seizures. **Severe physical withdrawal can be fatal and requires immediate medical attention at a hospital or medical treatment center.**

Another symptom of adolescent chemical dependency is **loss of control.** That is to say, when your child predetermines at what time and how much of a drug he is going to use, then violates those limits, he has lost his ability to control his usage. He might tell himself that he is going to drink one beer at a party and then finds himself drinking three beers because the compulsion to experience intoxication is triggered after drinking just the one beer. We often hear, "I planned for that bag of marijuana to last me all week, but it only lasted the weekend." Some adolescents who are addicted will try to quit but find that they use again and again. Perhaps, you have heard your child tell you that he will quit and *actually has* made an attempt to quit before. When you point out that he never truly quit he might respond with a terse, "I can quit if I want to!" This response is strictly a part of your child's denial about the strength of his dependence on drugs. Quitting drugs does not mean suspending usage; it means never using again. So, when a child continues to use despite having incurred unfavorable consequences, or if he has unsuccessfully attempted to cut his usage or quit altogether, these are symptoms that can be recognized as a part of chemical dependency. **It is impera-**

tive that you seek the help of a professional trained in addiction therapy and cessation to evaluate and diagnose your child. This discussion of characteristics is meant to provide you with awareness and information, *not* to use as a tool for you to diagnose your child.

Chapter 3

Community Enabling

Ryan left his progress report on the kitchen table before leaving to join his friends after school. He did not want to be at home when his parents saw his grades. They had been demanding to see his report card for days but Ryan, knowing that he had performed poorly, kept making excuses why he didn't have it so they would not prevent him from going out over the weekend. Finally, on Monday, he left his grades out for his parents to see. When his mother saw the progress report, her heart sank. She suspected the report would be worse than usual, but she was not prepared for three out of six failing marks. After speaking with her husband on the phone, she set up an appointment to meet with Ryan's teachers, school counselor and the vice principal. The meeting proved to be an eye opener. Ryan's parents were told that Ryan had "cut" at least two periods a day for the past two months. Ryan's first period teacher reported that when Ryan was in class, he would usually put his head down on his desk to sleep. To further complicate matters, his physical education teacher, who was also Ryan's football coach, admitted that he had given Ryan a passing grade to keep him eligible to play. Ryan's parents were outraged by the inaction of these school officials and the fact that they had not been informed about their son's behavior.

It's difficult to believe that people in positions of responsibility such as teachers, police, probation officers, judges, counselors and physicians, would knowingly allow an adolescent drug problem to continue. It does, in fact, happen. More frequently the case is that these same individuals, due to the lack of a thorough understanding of the causes of drug abuse and the dynamics that allow for its continuance, unwittingly and often with the best of intentions, make decisions that prolong or exacerbate a drug-abuse problem.

We have previously discussed denial as a prime factor that perpetuates a drug problem. Another key component that perpetuates drug use is enabling. **Enabling refers to the process by which others give to the drug-using individual the opportunity and the power to continue using drugs, thus preventing the user from experiencing the negative consequences of his actions.** Enabling detracts from or minimizes the consequences of drug-related behavior. Many institutions within our community exist for the growth, education, and protection of our children. These include schools, the legal system and counseling services. Community enabling occurs when the systems designed to help families, instead, make decisions that prevent the drug user from experiencing the full range of consequences associated with his drug use. This is not to say that every one of them enables all the time. However, it is a significant problem and while this chapter is not intended to place blame on individuals or institutions, it *is* intended to increase your awareness that all levels of authority can fail to deal directly and effectively with adolescent drug use. Several factors may contribute to your child's drug problem. These may include genetics, the possibility of biochemical disease and social and environmental conditions. In this chapter, we will focus on an environmental factor, community enabling.

It is not likely that an adolescent's involvement with drugs is a welcome and acceptable topic at the dinner table. Typically, your child has had to keep her drug use a secret from you because you would not have allowed her to continue to use. She would not have come to you after her first intoxication and said, "Guess what, Mom and Dad, I got drunk last night and liked it." She did not discuss her drug use and she continued to keep it a secret until she was caught. Unfortunately, her involvement with drugs was probably well underway long before you found out. You might have even asked yourself how it could have gone on this long without your knowledge. To keep you from finding out about her drug use, your child had to maintain a low profile, cover up unacceptable behavior or activities, lie and con. You had thought that the behavioral and attitudinal changes you saw were a normal part of adolescence. Perhaps your intuition suggested otherwise, but without evidence and the validation of people whose opinions we respect, it's difficult to act on a hunch. Sometimes we simply do not want to see a problem because we fear dealing with it.

Another reason that it took so long for your child's drug problem to be discovered is the issue of community enabling. Let's examine how this can occur at your child's school. We must preface this discussion with the fact that it makes no difference if your child attends public or private school, continuation or any other type of school. Chances are that enabling is happening within his school. Schools are comprised of people who have children's best interests at heart as well as those who have become complacent and do not want to get involved. Both types of individuals can enable your child's problems. For instance, teachers are the primary contacts that your child has during the school day. Sometimes, a teacher who genuinely cares about your child thinks that he is helping by refraining from expressing his concerns about your child's behavior to you. If this teacher senses that your child is having problems, he might believe that if he can get your child to open up and talk with him, he can help. However, if the teacher does not inform you about what is going on, he is keeping secrets that can have devastating results. Another reason that a teacher might not speak with you about your child's questionable behavior is that he thinks it is none of his business when a student sleeps during class or has frequent absences; delving in to the adolescent's life outside the classroom is beyond the scope of his responsibility. Additionally, some teachers might be taken in by the adolescent's "con." An example that clearly illustrates this is that of a student's "hard-luck" story about why her homework was not completed on time. If the teacher gives the student more time to finish the assignment without verifying the excuse, the teacher is buying into the student's attempt at manipulation.

The reality is that teachers have many students during the day. Their job is one that is filled with details and pressing matters. If your child is a student who stays out of trouble in the classroom, her teacher might not be as apt to contact you as he would be if your child was being disruptive or uncooperative. There are ways to counteract this type of enabling by enlisting the help of your child's teacher and the attendance office staff. If your child is

22

having trouble with his grades or with attendance, you should ask the teacher to send home weekly grade reports or ask the attendance office for weekly or daily verification of missed classes. Officials in the attendance office constantly monitor student absences. However, sometimes that office may not notify you of your child's lack of attendance until the problem has a significant impact on your student's academic performance. **A parent needs to be vigilant about her child's grades and class attendance.** We encourage you to enlist the help of your child's teachers in this manner; to create, in effect, a pro-active team effort to keep your child focused on the task at hand, her education.

Coaches, too, can enable athletes by making sure they receive a passing grade in physical education, even if they do not attend class, so that athletes remain eligible to play a particular team sport. They might simply "look the other way" at drug use, including the use of steroids or other performance-enhancing agents. Another way a coach can enable your child is by talking a teacher out of giving an athlete a failing grade. This way, your child will not become ineligible for the "big game" on Friday night.

The guidance counselors at your child's school are governed by strict education and confidentiality codes. Your adolescent might confide in her counselor about her drug use and the counselor might be quite concerned. However, the counselor must have reason to believe that your child or other students are in immediate danger or she must have explicit permission from the child herself in order to break a confidence. **We feel that individuals using drugs *are* in immediate danger.** If they are currently using drugs, or trapped in the progression of drug use, they and others will be vulnerable to harm. An experienced counselor, particularly one who possesses a thoroughgoing under-standing of the drug progression, may have the skills to intervene effectively. The counselor has the opportunity to encourage your child to be open and honest with you, to arrange a family meeting or to make an appropriate referral for drug counseling. However, the counselor's hands may be tied. Unfortunately, your adolescent will not be motivated to stop using just because the counselor knows about her involvement in drugs.

The role of the school counselor is to advise students about their academic challenges and offer encouragement and support for your child in this regard. Generally, they are trusted and admired by their students and are not considered disciplinarians. The revelation of a drug problem by a student to his counselor may indicate the child's own desire for help from a trusted, non-judgmental professional. It is likely that the child does not feel the freedom to approach his parents with this information and more likely, that he may fear the repercussions of his drug use. It is our strong opinion, however, that a drug problem kept secret is to no one's advantage and at the very least leaves the child in jeopardy. **It is imperative that you do your part to help your child by disclosing any concerns you have to your child's counselor.**

Sometimes a confusing, double message is sent to parents by school administrators concerning the drug-free image it hopes to promote. It may seem that a principal, for example, is dedicated to a drug-free school. She might promote drug awareness programs or maintain an active, *Friday Night Live*, group among students. She might arrange to have the accident-prevention program, *Every Fifteen Minutes*, presented to her students. She may invite speakers to campus to educate students about current drug issues. At the same time, she might be reluctant to identify a drug problem on her campus. To do so would serve as an admission that there is a drug problem in her school and she does not want to put her school's good reputation in question. An administrator's inability to acknowledge and deal with drug problems is much the same as the denial a parent experiences. If you admit that your child has a drug problem, you admit that it is a problem in your family. The reality is that keeping a student's drug problem secret only augments the problem. A healthy response would be that the principal refers the family immediately to the appropriate drug counselor as an initial step in the process of dealing with this problem. This situation demands cooperation and support both within the family and within the community.

A parent new to a child's junior or senior high school experience may view the role of the school's vice-principal as obscure. Vice-principals are usually the administrators to whom your child would be referred for a discipline problem, such as his being caught smoking cigarettes or marijuana or selling drugs on campus. They are most likely the people who would suspend your child or impose other disciplinary action. Sometimes, a student is suspended without having been referred to an appropriate source for help. Parents may not be informed if the vice-principal has suspicions that your child is using drugs on campus. Not revealing these suspicions to parents is remiss. However, one motive a vice-principal might have for failing to notify you with his concerns is the fact that he fears a parent's denial of his child's situation. They have probably heard on previous occasions indignant refutations from some parents such as, "No, not my child, you are mistaken," or "How dare you accuse my child of such a thing!" This behavior and response on behalf of the parent is at best frustrating and discouraging to the administrator. It is difficult to deal with a parent's denial. Nevertheless, an administrator's decision not to inform the parent of his impending disciplinary actions is a form of enabling. Any responsible attempt on the part of these school officials to confront a parent's denial of his child's drug problem should be deemed admirable regardless of a parent's response.

If you are not aware of the policies and procedures of your child's school or district, this is the time to ask the principal or vice-principal questions. You may want to inquire about how to become involved in the school. Are there committees on which you can serve? Offer to arrange to have experts in the field of adolescent chemical dependency speak to the faculty and students. Attend district board meetings. Your involvement will help acquaint you with the realities of current campus life and provide you with the opportunity to initiate programs or help to implement policies that might inhibit enabling behaviors.

We generally respect the wisdom and experience of physicians. We expect through their years of schooling and rigorous training that they've encountered a full spectrum of human problems. We assume that they possess compassionate natures. We have stated that a drug problem is a health issue, not a behavior problem. **The behaviors associated with drug use are a result of the drug use; not the cause of**

the drug use. The physician has the opportunity and responsibility to gather information about your child's health and to make a referral if drug use is apparent or suspected. Any health care assessment should include questions about drug use. Enabling occurs when the physician fails to make a referral because he did not want to break confidentiality. (Here, we are specifically speaking about patients under age 18.) Remember, a drug problem is a *health* issue. Your child's doctor would certainly tell you if your child had cancer. She would not consider that revelation a betrayal of confidentiality.

Dealing with an adolescent whom you suspect is using drugs can be confusing and sometimes frustrating. In your quest to discover what caused your wonderful child to change so drastically, you may have sought counseling from other professionals. In the event that you had no idea that your child was using drugs, you might have thought that she was upset about your divorce or was having trouble fitting in at school. Perhaps, you took her to a psychologist for treatment. The psychologist or other therapist could have inadvertently enabled your child by not asking direct questions regarding drug use. Your child might very well have emotional issues with which she must learn to cope. Until she stops using drugs, she cannot address the other issues in an effective, lasting way because she is currently medicating her feelings. These other problems will need to be explored. However, it is our experience and belief that treatment for the drug problem must come first. If your child's counselor does not ask about drugs, she is not getting a complete picture of your child.

Another way that a counselor might enable your child is by trying to treat the emotional issues first with the belief that the drug use will go away in the course of treatment. **Chemical dependency will not automatically disappear if behaviors and attitudes change.** We have evidence of this in our own practices.

For instance, a parent may become intensely focused on the child's out-of-control behavior and desperately seek help. Even if the parents know that the child is using drugs, their primary, immediate concern is that of the child's behavior. However, in an effort to change the behavior, they might send their child to a behavioral–modification, in-patient program. The program might discuss drug use but not treat it. The counselor-client discussions might include some education about drugs or even explore the emotional reasons for using drugs. Unless the program is one that promotes change by looking at the negative consequences of an individual's personal drug use and provides tools for maintaining on-going recovery within their home environ-ment, the child will likely emerge from the program with changed behaviors while still having a drug problem. This is due to the fact the adolescent's drug problem failed to be treated in a complete manner. With incomplete treatment, a teen returning to her home environment will usually, within a few weeks, return to using drugs.

The dynamics of community enabling are pervasive. Even the parents of your child's friends can play a part. There are parents who allow teenagers to drink in their homes. Some parents will allow teens to drink at anytime. Others allow drinking on special occasions, such as before a prom. Still others will allow teens to drink at parties they personally supervise. At that time, they may take car keys away from the teens to ensure that there will be no intoxicated adolescents behind the wheel of a car. These parents probably subscribe to the notion that teens are going to drink anyway, so it is better to allow them to do so under a parent's supervision. Unfortunately, that belief is a myth. It presumes that teens will not drink any place else or at any other time and reveals the parent's lack of insight that other drugs in addition to alcohol will be present on a specific occasion. These parents are not likely to inform the parents of children who are to be guests in their home that drinking will be allowed. Furthermore, some parents believe that smoking marijuana is harmless. There are parents who use drugs right along with their teenagers. This is extremely unhealthy behavior and strongly reinforces a child's belief that he does not have a drug problem.

The parents of your child's friends can also enable your child by providing room and board if your child has run away. This usually occurs with well-meaning adults who believe they are helping your child. After all, in using drugs, your child has become quite the manipulator and con artist. She might have told her friend's parents that you are unreasonable people who treat her very badly. They may feel sorry for her and want to help. They do not want your child to be out on the street and so will give her a warm and loving environment for the time being. These parents might not choose to call you to let you know that your child is safe and to ask your permission for her stay. After all, their perspective is probably that you are unreasonable. Your child certainly won't encourage communication between parents for fear of being caught in a lie.

The most powerful entity involved in community enabling is that of our legal system. This involves police, judges and probation officers. Most of us tend to believe that people in trouble with the law will finally receive the appropriate consequences for their negative behavior. Sometimes it is the last hope for an individual's rehabilitation or effort toward change. Individuals who work in law enforcement are often in positions that allow them to make decisions or order mandates which can have a significant impact on an adolescent who has a drug problem. Here are several examples in which children are allowed to escape opportunities for a legal intervention. Their factual basis was established as we worked with clients whose drug use continued because of these specific types of enabling.

In the first instance, the police might decide to forego giving your child a citation for possession of drugs when his car is pulled over, or for his loitering at the park or other public places. Perhaps, the officers break up a party of adolescents where drug use and drinking are occurring and allow the teens to leave without any consequences. At school dances, sporting events or other school activities they might be inclined to "look the other way" recalling their own youth and thinking that they're just kids having a few laughs. When an officer doesn't issue a ticket, arrest the offending adolescent or, at the very least, phone the teen's parents, the reality is that they are preventing that individual from experiencing the consequences of his own actions. With such leniency, a child's denial about his drug problem will be validated and made stronger.

Judges may too, enable adolescents by suspending sentences and by giving such light consequences that the teen is not affected by the outcome. Take for instance, the girl under the legal driving age who did not have a driver's license and was pulled over for "driving under the influence." The judge did not order mandatory counseling for drug and alcohol treatment, he simply *suggested* that she do that. He ordered that she could not have a driver's license until she turned eighteen. (Remember, not having a license did not stop her from driving before.) He fined her two hundred fifty dollars and required that she write a thousand-word essay about why her actions were wrong. Although he had the option of placing her on probation to hold her accountable, he chose not to. This judge had the opportunity to effectively intervene in this young woman's drug use but chose to "give her a break." Perhaps he did not understand that a drug problem requires that the user's denial of the problem be broken and that she must be made to accept the consequences of her actions. The sooner she realizes the impact her actions have on herself and others, the greater chance she will have at recovery. The failure of this judge to sentence this adolescent appropriately allowed her problem to continue and put her safety and the safety of others in jeopardy.

If your child is on probation, you might even find enabling behavior occurring within the probation department. A stipulation of the probation might be random drug testing by the probation officer. Testing is a mechanism to keep users honest about their use. Due to budget constraints within the department, the probation officer trying to manage costs might take your child's sample but not run the test. He may then tell your child that everything is fine. Your child may have actually used drugs only to be told that his test showed no use. Now the teen may think that his efforts to tamper with the drug test were successful. He may believe that he can continue to use drugs because he can beat the test. (Please note that most of the methods teenagers use to alter a drug test do not work.)

Occasionally, we have seen probation officers enable drug use by not checking up on a teenager often enough to make an impact on the child's denial of his problem. Many probation departments are understaffed. It might not be possible for them to regularly visit the individuals in their charge. Some adolescents are released from probation early as another method to handle work overload. This does not allow your child to experience the full consequences of his behavior. Court-mandated, regular supervision of an adolescent is an ever-present reminder to that individual that he must be accountable for finding resolution to a problem that is serious enough to render public scrutiny. In this way probation can be a very effective tool in helping adolescents to gain insight to their drug problem.

In every community, the many systems designed to protect and support families are subject to economic pressures and time constraints. It can be the case that key administrators are unaware of the nature and treatment of drug-use problems. Sometimes there is a significant lack of coordination among the various legal entities. These factors are disheartening. However, it is helpful to have realistic expectations and an awareness of their limitations if you and your child must confront any legal proceedings.

Chapter 4

Parental Denial and Enabling

When Mark began counseling two months ago, his parents thought they had caught his drug use early. They were aware of his occasional use of marijuana and alcohol; however, during Mark's weekend stay with his mother she became concerned when she overheard her son's phone conversation about how he would obtain beer for a party. She shared her concerns about Mark's part of the phone conversation with his father and stepmother. Mark's father's immediate response was that she was overreacting. Because Mark spent most of the time at his father and stepmother's house, Mark's dad conveyed with certainty the fact that Mark was just fine. He advised Mark's mother not to make an issue of this incident and assured her that all teenagers use drugs. Mark's mother was not convinced but decided to let the matter go.

A few weeks later Mark's report card arrived in the mail at his father's house. His grades had dropped to D's and F's. Alarmed, Mark's dad called the school only to find out that Mark had been cutting classes almost daily and was at risk of not graduating. The vice principal informed Mark's father that he believed Mark was using drugs and suggested he seek a professional evaluation for his son.

Mark's father was angry and confused. He decided to search Mark's room. He found a marijuana pipe in Mark's top dresser drawer. That evening, Mark's parents confronted him with their discovery. Mark was furious and defensive. He expressed indignation over his father's intrusion into his personal effects and fiercely denied that he had a problem with drugs in spite of his ready admission that he smoked marijuana and drank alcohol at parties. He told his parents that they were making a big deal about nothing. Although his parents believed that Mark did not have a serious drug problem they decided to have him evaluated. Mark was in jeopardy of not graduating with his high school class and his parents worried that if that happened, it would further undermine his already fragile self-esteem. They agreed that it would be in their son's best interest to clear the unexcused absences that he had accumulated over the semester.

After two months of counseling, Mark's parents discovered that his drug problem was more extensive than they had realized or had been willing to admit. The example of Mark's family is one that is frequently communicated by the clients we serve in our practice. That same example, too, demonstrates the power of the defense mechanism, denial, in both the individual using drugs and parents who must accept and cope with the revelation of their child's problem. Revelations such as those stated in the example can help parents to observe ways in which they have contributed to their child's ongoing problem. Ideally, parents must recognize that by "rescuing" their adolescent, they are enabling, not helping their child. Rescuing refers to the behaviors used by others (i.e. parents) that prevent or forestall an individual from experiencing the full range of consequences that accompany his drug use. Just as community enabling can hinder your child's and your family's recovery, some of your own behaviors and attitudes may get in the way of your child's recognition that drug use is a problem in his life.

When a person or family is in crisis, as you might be with your child who is using drugs, two of the most common ways to respond to problems are to deny and enable. Both of these responses reflect codependent ways of behaving. Melody Beattie, the author of *Codependent No More*, states the definition of codependent as, "one who has let another person's behavior affect him or her, and who is obsessed with controlling that person's behavior".[1] Parents who are codependent are generally quick to react emotionally to problems and forego choosing responses that include a calm approach and the subsequent application of logical consequences to their child's negative behavior. For instance, say your daughter is supposed to have her room in order by three o'clock, Saturday afternoon, if she wants to go out that evening. You may notice at one-thirty that her bed is not made, the waste can is full and dirty clothes are strewn on the floor. To no avail, you may remind her or coax her to take care of her room. By three, the chore has failed to be completed. Instead of letting it go and calmly waiting for her to demonstrate the fact that she intends to go out anyway, you might yell and scream, citing all her bad qualities. In an emotional tirade, you might call her selfish, unorganized and lazy. However, there is no need for any of that. When your daughter appears at your side at six o'clock that evening asking for the keys to the car, you then have the opportunity to quietly remind her that she did not fulfill her duties. She may express her disappointment (perhaps, dramatically) and that's okay. Ignore it. It is likely that the following Saturday her room will be cleaned early in the day.

You have been affected in many ways by your child's behaviors resulting from her drug use. There might have been ways that you have tried to "help" your child but, unwittingly, have kept her from seeing the reality of the consequences of her drug use. Perhaps, you have attempted to control her behavior rather than helping her towards getting drug free. You have inadvertently impeded her road to independence and maturity as well. Part of the goal of parenting is to help your child to become responsible for her actions and to accept the consequences of her behavior. The following discussion will illustrate many of the common ways parents participate in their own denial and enabling of their child's drug problem. It is helpful, albeit necessary, to become acquainted and familiar with these behaviors in an effort to increase your awareness about your own role within a family that is coping with an adolescent drug problem.

Minimizing the reality and the seriousness of an adolescent's problem with drugs is an attitude and outlook that helps to convince a parent that the situation at hand is not as bad as it looks or sounds. These parents reason that any given set of circumstances could always be worse. One parent might tell herself that because her son maintains good grades or never breaks a curfew, he certainly could not be involved with drugs. Another mother consoles herself with gratitude that her son is not in a gang. Frequently, a parent will insist that because her child participates in a sports program he will be precluded from using chemicals. The mixture of sports and drugs does not make sense. One is a health-building activity while the other is a health-destroying activity. The reality in these scenarios is that it is possible for a child to do all of these activities and still be involved in drugs. Drug use can continue for quite some time before it is dramatically apparent or significantly interferes with the child's performance at school or with her home life. Minimizing is a powerful device that can effectively postpone the end to a problem while simultaneously causing a problem to become more complicated or increase in severity.

Avoidance can be described as "looking for answers in all the wrong places." As a part of your personal denial system, you may not be willing to accept the fact that your child has a drug problem, nevertheless, you continue to have a nagging sense that "something" is not right. As an attempt to quell your concerns and, hopefully, shed some light on the current set of circumstances, you might take your child to a counselor to rule out the possibility of depression or other emotional issues. It's entirely possible that your child *does* experience depression or suffer from a mental health illness. However, not having your child assessed for a possible drug problem is an effort to side step that issue. Parents have a responsibility to examine the issue of drug use as closely as they would their child's academic performance, health or safety issues, preferably, *before* there is a problem.

Avoidance is also displayed by not wanting to "rock the boat." If your child's behaviors and attitudes have been tolerable lately, you probably do not want to confront her for fear that you will evoke turmoil. The absence from turbulent behaviors associated with her drug use has been a nice change for the members of your household, so why spoil it by telling her you are taking her to counseling? The reason to take her to counseling now and not postpone that option is that the state of "peace" you might be currently experiencing is only temporary. The turmoil will return.

Blaming oneself or others serves as a great detractor from the problem at hand. As long as you are accepting the blame for the problems your child is experiencing or placing the blame on others, you then keep yourself from focusing on what is truly important: helping your child to get drug free. While it is true that different systems and people might have *enabled* your child to use drugs, they are not to *blame* for his drug use. When you blame others for your child's problem, you cause yourself to feel like a victim. You may feel that you lack the power to change what is happening. That same feeling of helplessness can further cause you to feel "stuck" in the situation. Blaming keeps you locked in that perception. In order for positive change to occur, it is important to direct your efforts away from blaming a person or system to focusing on the child's drug problem. Focusing on the problem of drug use allows you to explore ways to move forward and work toward a solution to the problem.

Often we find that within a family much of the blame of a child's drug problem will fall on one or the other parent. This can happen when one parent has been a strict disciplinarian while the other has been more lenient. "If you weren't so hard on him" or "you allow too much freedom" are common blaming statements. Your child uses this division between his parents to his advantage by working one parent against the other. This can occur in "intact" families or in families that have experienced divorce. In divorced families, one parent may insist that the child live at his residence because the other parent has failed to successfully raise their child. This blaming behavior is destructive, particularly to the child, and postpones any chance for problem solving.

Accepting the "con" means that you accept, without question, an individual's explanation or rationale for a particular situation that occurred even though their explanation may seem improbable. Parents want to believe the things that their children tell them. They do not want to accept the fact that their child could look them straight in the eyes and lie! An example of a lie you might have heard from your child is that her eyes are red from allergies. When you've found marijuana or a pipe in your child's backpack he might deny it is his and explain that he is holding it for a friend. If you accept this without question or without verifying that information, you are buying into the con. These are tactics that drug users employ to avoid being "busted" (found out). Your daughter might get tearful or defensive that you think she even would do such a thing! You love your child and previously she never lied to you. Therefore, you tell her that you believe her and perhaps feel guilty for doubting her, but deep inside you know she is not telling the truth. **Trust your instincts and intuition**. The nature of drug use is that your child has to lie in order to protect her relationship with the drugs.

Ignoring advice can ensure that your child will continue his drug use. A friend, relative, teacher, school administrator or others might have told you that they have seen changes in your child. They might not have come right out and said they believe that your child is using drugs, they more likely implied it. Maybe you chose to get defensive or to ignore their words. Perhaps another parent called and said his own child has been using and your child hangs around with her. You chose to ignore that warning sign and to believe that your child is smarter than that. A teacher might call and say your child has been sleeping in class or her grades have dropped. You rationalized that she is tired due to her involvement in sports.

The above examples are just a few that depict the extent of the use of denial behaviors. Our purpose in sharing them is to get you thinking about ways in which you have been in denial about your child's drug use. Our purpose is *not* to trigger guilt and shame. Denial must be recognized and admitted before an individual can clearly see the truth of a situation. Denial protects us from facing our fears as well as other emotions. It might help to write down the ways in which you use denial or the situations that evoke your denial. This will help you to identify and recognize its presence in your everyday life so that you can make a choice to relinquish this behavior. Use this awareness as a tool for change.

Here are important things to understand before further discussion of our four remaining examples of enabling. Enabling detracts from or minimizes the consequences of chemically-related behavior. When you prevent the drug user from experiencing the full range of consequences associated with his chemical use, you unintentionally distort his already distorted picture of reality. This allows his denial system to remain intact. It is imperative that he knows what his chemical use is doing to himself and others. You do not want your child to experience pain and want to protect him. However, when it comes to drug abuse or addiction, **if your child does not experience the consequences of his use, he will not see any reason to quit**. In this subject area, pain motivates change. Therefore, it is vital to his recovery that you recognize the ways you have been unintentionally enabling him to continue his use. You must allow him to experience the consequences. This is difficult at times, because your instincts tell you to protect him. The question becomes, "Am I protecting or am I enabling him?" The following are four examples of enabling behaviors that do not help or protect your child:

Rescuing: You do not want to see your child fail or sink deeper into trouble. It is enough of a struggle to deal with her drug use. One example of how you might be rescuing is writing excuses for classes she has cut. You might know she is cutting classes to get high, but you don't want her to get into trouble at school. You fear she is at risk of not graduating from high school or being placed in continuation high school so you clear her cuts. You might think you are protecting her but in reality you are not allowing her to experience the consequence of cutting classes. She will not be able to relate the consequence to her drug use. Other ways of rescuing are:

1) Making excuses to teachers, relatives or friends for your child's chemically-related behavior.

2) Paying off drug debts because you are afraid of what might happen to your child if you don't.

3) Doing her chores for her because you are sick of fighting and nagging about it.

4) Doing her homework for her.

5) Hiring a lawyer to defend her D.U.I. or other drug offense.

Parents who engage these behaviors cause an adolescent to believe that drug use is a positive thing. It's almost as if she has a partner in her drug use. Certainly, she cannot see any reason to stop. She has her parents in her service and covering all the bases, taking up the slack in her life.

Bargaining is another form of enabling. One of the ways you might bargain is to say to yourself, "If he is going to drink, I'd rather have him do it at home." This might sound reasonable; however, as you have read in previous chapters, any drug use by an adolescent is harmful. This also sends your child a double message that drinking is okay under certain circumstances, such as drinking at home, but not under others, such as parties where parents are not present. Another bargaining behavior is "I won't tell your father/mother this time, but if it ever happens again..." This only divides the united front that parents need to present to the child. If they can, drug users will manipulate their parents.

One final bargaining behavior that enables your child is promising to give her something if she will stop using drugs. Parents may think they can entice their adolescent to stop using drugs with the offer of a new car, an extravagant trip or new clothes. This seems like it would be great motivation to stop. However, when it comes to addiction, bargaining does not work. Remember that your child has developed a relationship with the drugs that is probably stronger than any other relationship in her life. Therefore, as much as she would like to quit for that car she is unable to do so. Instead of the car being an incentive to change, the car could become a symbol of her failure because the drug problem that has developed in her life leaves her without the necessary tools to make those changes even if she desperately wants the car.

"Stuffing" feelings is a dynamic that occurs over time as you find yourself less inclined to express your true feelings to your child concerning the matter of her drug use and the problems that it continues to cause. This might come about as a result of the increase in your child's disrespectful attitude, behaviors or verbal abuse towards you and others. Perhaps you have not said anything for fear you will be rejected by her seemingly, "I don't care" attitude. Stuffing your feelings is a normal reaction to pain. You might think that your daughter really doesn't care how you feel, so there is no point in showing or expressing your feelings and risking getting hurt by her response. Although she appears not to care about your feelings anymore, it is nevertheless critical that you express your feelings honestly. She needs to know that you are hurt and disappointed when she swears at you. She needs to know you were afraid that she was in a car wreck when she was late for her curfew. By not expressing your feelings you are not allowing her to experience the consequences of her drug use. The way you feel about her and the things she says and does to you *do* have an affect on her.

You may withhold your feelings from your spouse, "significant other", extended family or close friends. There is still a great deal of social stigma attached to drug use. For this reason, you might be reluctant to share your family's problem with drugs with the people closest to you. It can be difficult to express how you are feeling about your child's problem and you may fear that you will be judged or criticized. If you are completely at a loss as to what course of action to take regarding the drug problem, confiding in individuals who are not professionals in a position to help you is a risk you may not find prudent to take. However, isolating yourself is not healthy. It is essential that you get support for yourself at this time.

Increasing tolerance for intolerable behavior refers to the erosion of standards that were previously adhered to in your home. Because you are tired of constant battles with your child or other family members, you might begin to ignore behaviors that, prior to the presence of a drug problem, used to be unacceptable. For example, you might tolerate louder and louder stereo volume rather than risk a confrontation or fight with your child. You might allow curfew violations to continue without consequences. Verbal abuse and language that was not acceptable in the past, might now be grudgingly endured. Perhaps these seem like small issues compared to the drug issue itself. However, they are all a part of the same problem and need to be treated as such. For a while, there may be increased tension in your home life as you begin to reintroduce consequences for your child's behavior or begin to utilize consequences for the first time. This is to be expected and is a part of the process of encouraging change in your child. To help you manage issues such as those stated above, in chapter five, we will provide details of how to implement our *Setting Limits Contract*. The purpose of the *Setting Limits Contract* is to create a structure that will cause your child to maintain accountability for his actions. Following the guidelines of the contract will make it increasingly more difficult for your child to continue her drug use.

Parenting under the best conditions is difficult. Parenting an adolescent with a drug problem is incredibly more complicated. There are many resources available to assist you in your desire to understand and solve problems associated with your child's drug use. Chemical use by any member of a family becomes a family matter. Each person is affected by the use. Likewise, recovery from chemical dependency is a family issue! Every member of a family must pursue his own healing process. We must emphasize the fact that your child has a much greater chance of life-long recovery if you are willing to initiate your own recovery process. Your child's recovery is not a matter of dropping him at a counselor's offices or treatment facility hoping that the drug counselor will repair your child. Without your support and hard work, chances are slim that he will be successful in his recovery.

Chapter 5

Setting Limits for Your Child

Helping an adolescent to seek recovery from a drug problem is a process that involves several steps. It must be emphasized that at the time this problem is unveiled, everyone in the individual's family is henceforth involved in that person's attempt to get drug-free. It is essential that all members must work on their individual recovery from the effects of their loved one's drug use. Furthermore, we cannot stress enough the importance and the necessity of the recovery process for those individuals (i.e. parents) who may also have chemical dependency problems. Recovery means abstaining from the use of chemicals as well as working to change the behaviors, thinking and attitudes that keep a person using. When you hear "RECOVERY," think "CHANGE!"

Four important steps that facilitate an individual's early recovery are:

1) Recognition and admission that a drug problem exists;

2) A thorough understanding of the progress- sion of drug use and the awareness of devices such as denial and enabling that serve to undermine recovery;

3) Enlisting support from the appropriate professional counselor(s)and community resources; and

4) Intervention.

Intervention refers to the specific, concrete actions that are taken to impede an individual's drug use and actions that are taken which allow a child to experience immediate consequences when he or she uses drugs. Two critical and overriding components that make this process work are **unification** and **perseverance** on the part of the parties tending to the needs of the drug-using adolescent. This generally includes (but is certainly not limited to) parents and stepparents. When parents face that fact that their child is using drugs, they commonly experience feelings of powerlessness, frustration and resentment. They are understandably afraid for their child's welfare and afraid that they might not be able to solve this problem. As the parent and provider for your child, you have the right to expect her to behave within certain limits; additionally, you have the responsibility to communicate those limits clearly. Part of your child's responsibility is being aware of those behavioral expectations and the consequences of choosing not to meet them. On the following page, we present a model that we have developed to aid parents in setting healthy limits on their child's behavior. This model is titled the *Setting Limits Contract.* Its implementation will be an important first step in the intervention process. Successful implementation of this model will come from the careful development of its provisions with your child's counselor and their subsequent enforcement. You should be aware that your child might resent the use of this instrument and, like all children, will test its limits to determine if you are serious. The presentation of the model is followed by a detailed explanation of its intent and appropriate use.

Setting Limits Contract

Expectations for:

<u>Recovery</u>

1) Maintain abstinence from all drugs, alcohol and nicotine.

2) Follow through with random drug testing.

   * Tampering with a test or refusal to test is considered a positive test.

   * Initiating honesty about using drugs will incur a less severe consequence than a failure to meet Expectation #1.

3) Follow through with the counselor's recommendations.

4) Attend all scheduled counseling appointments.

5) Successfully complete a drug-treatment program.

Home

1) Follow the curfew guidelines.

2) Complete chores by a specified time.

3) Participate in family activities.

4) Allow no drugs on the property.

School

1) Show up for all classes on time.

2) Complete all homework.

3) Follow through with the rules of behavior at school.

4) Maintain an acceptable grade point average (GPA).

Other

1) Do not get into a car when the driver has used any drugs/alcohol.

Consequences for Unmet Expectations:

Recovery

1.

2.

3.

4.

5.

Home

1.

2.

3.

4.

5.

School

1.

2.

3.

4.

5.

Other

SETTING LIMITS CONTRACT

Working Model

Effective Recovery Example:

Expectation	Consequences
• Abstain from all drugs, alcohol and nicotine.	• Grounded for 14 days.
• Follow through with drug testing. ➢ *Tampering with a test or refusal to take a test is considered a dirty test.* ➢ *Drug tests are to come back negative.*	• Grounded for 14 days.
• Successfully complete a drug treatment program.	• College tuition, room and board will be rescinded.
• Adhere to a curfew of 10:00 p.m. on weekdays and 12:00 a.m. on weekends.	• Your curfew is two hours less the next evening that you go out. *(If this occurs for two consecutive days, then you are grounded for one day.)*

Ineffective Recovery Example:

Expectation	Consequences
• Stop using drugs	• You will spiral deeper into physical and emotional turmoil, ruining your health and stunting your growth
• Take drug tests	• You will spiral deeper into physical and emotional turmoil, ruining your health and stunting your growth
• Follow the counselor's recommendations	• You will not improve or resolve your problems

The *Setting Limits Contract* is not meant to control your child but to maintain a well-defined structure in which your child can be held accountable for the choices he makes. Having to submit immediately to a corresponding consequence for an unmet behavioral expectation will make it increasingly difficult for your child to continue his drug use. The contract sets boundaries and states consequences in advance, so there are no surprises during emotional times. By building into a parent's disciplinary program the element of consistency, the contract serves as a valuable tool for parents who used to lose sleep wondering what to do with their child who continued to use drugs, stayed out late, skipped classes at school and neglected his responsibilities at home. In addition to their parents, our adolescent clients have also discovered many benefits using the contract. Regarding lack of consistency, one of our clients expressed that, "Some days my mom will not care if I skip my math class. She might get upset or nag me a bit. Other days she grounds me. I get frustrated and angry because I don't know what she wants from me." Of course, what she wants is for her son to attend all classes! However, because this mother's response to her son missing his classes varies at different times it is understandably difficult for him to follow her direction. Her inconsistent responses make it difficult to know if she is serious about wanting her child to make positive changes in his behavior.

This frustration is exacerbated if a child is getting inconsistent messages about expectations and consequences from not only one parent but the other parent(s) as well. Often, there are four parents to whom the child must answer. Many children suffer from not knowing what is expected. This can creates stress, anxiety, confusion and rebellion. Lack of unity or consensus concerning which expectations are reasonable and which consequences can be exercised with consistency may create the same negative feelings among parents. Getting two separate households to act uniformly in this matter is even more challenging. The *Setting Limits Contract* will eliminate the nagging and stress that are sometimes associated with a parent's attempt to get her child to complete chores or tend to other responsibilities. It is *your* job to work closely with your child's counselor to develop, implement and follow through with the *Setting Limits Contract*.

There are three overriding principles that govern the execution of the *Setting Limits Contract*. They are as follows:

1) There must be logical consequences for unmet expectations.

2) Parents must be willing to follow through with the predetermined consequences.

3) Parents must work together.

Within your family structure, there must be logical consequences for unmet expectations. The expectations that you consider to be most important must have the most severe consequences. That is to say, the consequence for not doing the dishes should be less severe than the consequence for using drugs. When you are formulating the consequences, we recommend that grounding never be longer than three weeks because an adolescent perceives any amount of time longer than that as eternity! A lengthy grounding might seem to you that you are sending a strong message that a particular behavior will not be tolerated. Rather, it tends to create a climate for rebellion, defiance and acting-out behavior. Most people, especially youngsters, are sensitive to unfairness. They are able to differentiate between a consequence that is appropriate and a consequence that is illogical and has become a protracted means for an authority figure to express his or her personal frustration. We all like to be treated with fairness and this must always be a consideration when establishing consequences.

As many parents discover, formulating consequences is a difficult part of your role in the intervention process. It is primarily difficult because it is unfamiliar. However, learning how to establish consequences by understanding their purpose and their logical connection to stated expectations will help to dispel any apprehension. Working with your child's counselor will be helpful in clarifying the particular needs of your child. Furthermore, it is very important to have the opportunity to listen to other parents who have effectively applied the expectations/logical consequences concept in their own households, as well as, listening to parents who are struggling to learn how to do this for the first time. This can be accomplished by attending the community support group called, *ToughLove*®. (See www.ToughLove.com for more information.) We are strong proponents of this nationally known group whose purpose is to offer parents support, knowledge, awareness and techniques for holding children accountable for their actions. As counselors, we can provide you with information regarding discipline and consequences for negative behavior. The people in *ToughLove*® can provide you with peer support. When attending these meetings, you will hear stories similar to the ones your own family has experienced. Parents new to the program can garner helpful ideas and become aware of a range of behavior in both children and adults. Help offered by those people experiencing the same challenges as one's own can be quite meaningful. Don't let the group's name frighten you or put you off. Remember, when it comes to helping your child get drug-free: **Toughness without love is abuse, and love without**

toughness is enabling. Your child's counselor can refer you to the schedule of meetings in your area or you can obtain the group's phone number from the white or yellow pages.

The second key principle in exercising the *Setting Limits Contract* is that parents must be willing to follow through with the predetermined consequences. A consequence is not a consequence if you cannot fully implement it. If you do not think you will follow through with grounding your child for two weeks, then do not put it on the contract as a consequence. **It is crucial to your parenting and the intervention process that you only have consequences on the contract that you will implement to the fullest.** This requires you to take an honest look at what you are willing to do. Consider the following questions: If you ground your child, will you be grounding yourself as well? If you take away your daughter's driver's license for a week, will you be able to get her to school or to work? Every parent will need to do things a bit differently, tailoring consequences to meet the needs of his or her particular family. It will depend, in large part, on the child's age. Children over eighteen years will require treatment specific to that age and their younger counterparts will require their own age-appropriate treatment. Reconcile the fact that some consequences might be too difficult to implement. Keep in mind appropriate consequences that motivate change and encourage abstinence from drugs. Keep your sights on your goal: **Your child's recovery.**

When your child experiences consequences for unmet expectations, he will see that you are following through with your duties implied by the contract. He will realize that he needs to make changes in his behavior because the behaviors used previously will not continue to work. If you threaten consequences and fail to follow through with them, you will send your child the message you are not serious about your expectations. Being inconsistent with the expectations and consequences will not only sabotage the intervention process, it will become a source of stress and frustration in your family. You will feel powerless and your child will feel that she has all the control. **Threatening behavior is enabling behavior and following-through behavior is healthy parenting and intervention.**

The third principle required in exercising the contract is to determine which consequences that can be mutually agreed upon by all parents or individuals who have custodial rights. Arriving at a consensus among several people can prove to be quite challenging and there are several factors that can make this process difficult.

Your child, like every drug user, is a manipulator. This may sound harsh to you. It is the case, however, that individuals use manipulative tactics when they are not able to acquire their needs in a direct, honest manner. Drug involvement is laden with secrecy and deception. One common maneuver involves a child's attempt to divide two parents by setting up an alliance between her and one of her parents. For example, an adolescent will try to convince one parent that it is in that parent's best interest to keep her (the adolescent's) drug use a secret. She might say something like, "Dad has had a very hard day at work, Mom, and your telling him that I smoked marijuana today will only make his day harder." Parents who buy into their child's "conning" by keeping secrets from the other parent only enable their child to continue using.

In addition to manipulation, you might notice that you and your spouse or the other parents have vastly different viewpoints concerning the realm of expectations and consequences for your child's behavior. One partner may see the other's disciplinary actions toward their child as too strict. The partner who is offended by the other's behavior might compensate by being lenient towards their child. This is a situation that can easily escalate emotionally and can cause increasing division between parents. When parents are *polarized* (by that, we mean parents who maintain opposing extremes of viewpoints) about expectations and consequences, the adolescent quickly recognizes dissension. If you tell yourself or the other parents that you or they are too strict or too lenient, then this is a sign that polarization is probably present in the dynamics of your relationship. Again, this is a divisive mechanism and one that can be used by the adolescent to manipulate a situation.

The *Setting Limits Contract* will impede some of your child's attempts at manipulation and facilitate closing the gap on differing viewpoints of expectations and consequences. You must continually ensure that you have not left your adolescent a way to come between you and the other parent or parents. She will try to test these relationships to her own advantage. **It is imperative to the intervention process that all parents work together as a united team and that all households use one contract.** We suggest, if there are two households, either all parents get together and develop the contract from the start, or you each develop your own contract and present it to each other. Make the needed revisions until there is one final contract. We recommend that this process be facilitated by your child's counselor. Having your child's counselor's involvement in this process will ensure that all parents stay focused on the preparation of a contract that is in your child's best interest.

Look at the *Setting Limits Contract* provided at the beginning of this chapter and the page titled, "Effective and Ineffective Examples of Setting Limits Contract." We have provided the majority of the expectations needed to intervene in your child's drug use. Keep in mind when reviewing the *Setting Limits Contract* that school may include college if your child is over 18 years old and financially dependent on you. We use these expectations with all of the families with whom we work because these specific expectations make it increasingly difficult for adolescents to use drugs and manipulate the family structure. The expectations we listed are very clear. **Clarity is crucial**. Like a good attorney, your child will find any loopholes inherent in a vaguely constructed contract. Where you see the letters A., B., etc., underneath the numbers, add only one or two more expectations as they apply to your family. Creating an exhaustive list of expectations will dilute the importance of the ones we have listed for you. It is important to understand that intervention is a component of treatment and is not a punishment or an attempt to create "the perfect child."

In the following discussion, we will specify the significance of the expectations listed on the model. In the recovery column under the heading "Expectations for Recovery":

1) *Maintain abstinence from all drugs, alcohol and nicotine.*

If you simply write abstinence from all drugs as an expectation on the contract, your child might continue to drink alcohol because she might not yet understand that alcohol is a drug. It is the most widely abused substance among adolescents and young adults. **Remember that drug abuse or addiction is not about the drug. It is about intoxication.** Although the side effects may be different, the symptoms and consequences experienced are the same for alcohol as they are for other drugs. We include nicotine because this drug has the highest rate of addiction in our society. In 1997, the Centers for Disease Control and Prevention (CDC) reported that more people die from nicotine addiction each year than from all of the other drugs, auto accidents and HIV combined.[1] Many of the adults who are struggling with their nicotine addiction started as adolescents. According to Elizabeth Stuyt, people who are required to abstain from nicotine while they abstain from other drugs have a higher success rate of recovery than those who continue to smoke.[2] People in treatment for their drug problem who are told they can continue to use nicotine relapse twice as often than those required to abstain from nicotine. We view continued nicotine use for people in treatment as a huge relapse risk factor. It sabotages your child's recovery if you enable your child's nicotine use while you are asking her to stop the other drugs. Finally, according to Dr. Richard Hurt's research in 1996, more alcoholic individuals die from tobacco related diseases than they do from alcoholism.[3]

2) *Follow through with random drug testing.*

As we have mentioned throughout this book, drug-using adolescents lie, con, and manipulate to cover up and protect their drug use. You have probably already experienced this when your child lied to you about her drug use in the past. She might still be lying to you. As counselors, we are lied to as well. Drug-users lie to protect their relationship with intoxication. One thing we have learned over the years is drug tests do not lie when proper specimen collection protocol is followed. Therefore, the second expectation in the recovery column concerns drug testing.

The methods of drug testing include using samples of urine, blood or hair. Urine analysis testing is not only easy; it also supplies the most current information. It is imperative that you and your child's counselor know what drugs he is using. There are specific elements of treatment necessary for a person's use of each individual drug. While your child might be telling you he has been smoking marijuana, he might be hiding the fact that he is using LSD, methamphetamine, cocaine, vicodin, alcohol or other drugs. The certainty can only be obtained by drug testing. Please refer to our website: http://www.newdirectionsprogram.com

Drug testing needs to be random. If you let your child know he will be drug tested next week, then he will know he can get drunk or high tonight because any remnant of drugs might be out of his system by then. Your child should not know when he is going to be drug tested. One of the statements we have heard from many teens is, "After my dad drug tests me, I go out and get high, because I know I won't be tested for at least a week." We encourage you to occasionally take a urine sample from your child on Friday night and let him think you are submitting it to the lab. Throw it away. Then test him again on Saturday or Sunday morning to get an accurate sample that truly measures if he is using drugs.

There are many businesses marketing themselves as drug-detection agencies. You will want to talk with your child's counselor to find out which agency is the best and where it is located in your community. Some counselors even do drug testing themselves. Now that you have an awareness of the significance of drug testing you have to make sure your child has not tampered with the drug test.

2A) *Tampering with a test or refusal to test is considered a positive test (same consequence as expectation #1).*

A positive test means drugs are present in your child's body. When you ask for a urine sample from your child he might refuse. In this case, you simply want to implement the consequence. There is no need to fight with your child and stress yourself out about this, simply implement the consequence and let the other parents and your child's counselor know the situation so everyone is aware.

Over the years we have learned from our adolescent clients about tampering with drug tests. For instance, your child might use a friend's urine. This happens quite often. He will use a urine sample from a friend and pour it into the cup when he is being tested. He will add water, bleach or other products to the urine sample. Because there may be attempts to compromise the test it is important that you or another parent of the same sex be present with your child while he is testing. One tool you can use to determine if he has used another person's urine or added water to a urine sample is to use an inexpensive digital thermometer. After you have taken the urine sample check the temperature. It should be close to 98.6 degrees. If it is greater than 99 degrees then you have to check to see if your child has a fever. If he doesn't have a fever then you know he has tampered with the test. Absolutely do not accept a urine sample under 96 degrees, because any temperature under 96 degrees most likely indicates your child has tampered with the urine sample. You can always collect another sample if it is less than 96 degrees. To order drug detection kits and learn more about the protocol for proper drug testing, you can visit Drug Detection Laboratories, Inc. at http://www.drugdetection.net. You can also email their toxicologist at director@drugdetection.net. They are prompt when responding to their emails.

People used to think if they drank cranberry juice or vinegar it would flush drugs from their system so they would not test positive for drugs. The rationale was that marijuana sticks to fat cells in the body and that vinegar would consume the fat as well as the detectable marijuana. Currently, some people think a dietary supplement, "Goldenseal", will mask the presence of drugs in the body's system or taking niacin will somehow eliminate marijuana from the fat cells. There are other products in magazines and health food stores that are marketed as products that will guarantee a negative drug test. While these techniques are not effective, it is the case that some tests are more sensitive than others are. New Directions (our counseling program, http://www.newdirectionsprogram.com) uses tests from Drug Detection Laboratories, Inc (http://www.drugdetection.net) which tests as few as 15 nanograms of marijuana in the system. Other tests only go as low as 50 nanograms. We have seen many cases where a child has tested over 100 nanograms (the upper limit cut off) and ten days later test negative or below 15 nanograms (the lower limit cut off). Even a very sensitive drug test often detects marijuana for about ten days in a young person's body.

There are some products costing twenty-five to thirty dollars each whose manufacturers claim that they are effective in masking the presence of drugs in the body for a five-hour period. We do not know the accuracy of the claim but five hours is not a very long period of time for that price! Because they are expensive, some of our clients have told us they steal these products. A toxicologist pointed out to the counselors in our program that these products will not work with random drug testing because random drug testing allows the parent to control the time at which his or her child will be tested.

2B) *Initiating honesty about using drugs is a less severe consequence than expectation #1.*

Honesty about drug use means your child comes to you after using and says, "Mom, I messed up." If you were about to drug test your child and he then says, "Oh yeah, I need to be honest with you, I got high last night," that is *not initiating* honesty. That example reveals that your child has been cornered and that you are about to find out the truth through drug testing. Initiating honesty happens when your child comes to you of his own volition to disclose his drug use. Remember, even though he is coming to you and being open, he still must experience a consequence for using. Not implementing a consequence would send a message to your child that all he has to do is tell you about his drug use and nothing will happen. We suggest the consequence be less severe than that for violating expectation #1 in the contract.

1) *Follow through with the counselor's recommendations.*

Your child's counselor will have recommendations geared toward helping your child get sober and into recovery and will need leverage to make sure the recommendations are carried out. The counselor might recommend that your child attend *Narcotics Anonymous* or *Alcoholics Anonymous* or smoking-cessation classes. He or she might assign therapeutic homework or some other task. If your child is not held accountable for the recommendations of his counselor he might not be inclined to complete the various tasks assigned. Failure to follow through with his counselor's recommendations enables him to not work toward his recovery. Counselors must have the support and force of the contract.

2) *Attend all scheduled counseling appointments.*

We have mentioned that your child is not supposed to want to take an open and honest look at his relationship with drugs and instantly quit. Your child has an illness and needs treatment in which he can't participate alone. Therefore, it is imperative that he attend all scheduled appointments. He might come up with a variety of excuses for why he doesn't want to go. For example: "It's my Friday, school got out early today, I want to go skating." The illness your child has does not go on break when school is out for Christmas or summer. Actually, a significant relapse risk factor for adolescents is their having too much time on their hands. Your child needs structure. Following through with scheduled counseling appointments and honoring commitments will augment and fortify this necessary structure.

3) *Successfully complete a drug treatment program.*

Your child's counselor may recommend inpatient treatment. After his discharge from the inpatient treatment program, the contract should be implemented as part of his aftercare program.

Successful completion of a drug treatment program is to be determined by your child's counselor, **not by your child**. Your child might stay clean for sixty days and skillfully articulate to you that he is fully "recovered" and ready to stay clean in his community of drug-using friends. This might be a manipulation on your child's part or simply his denial about the severity of his illness. The counselor will need to determine when your child has completed all that has been asked of him. Working with his counselor in a program of recovery, your child will be required to take a look at his drug problem. He will be encouraged to be honest with you about his drug problem. He will learn to develop a "feelings" vocabulary to explore his emotions. By this we mean that he will learn to identify *specific* feelings such as anger, rejection or anxiety rather than identifying his feelings as a broad, emotional experience such as, "I feel pissed off or I feel okay." Being specific about his feelings is an important step that will help him to cope with his emotions. He will be asked to make changes in his behavior and he will be encouraged to make changes in his social life. If he is chemically dependent he will be encouraged to develop an association with *Twelve-Step* groups such as Alcoholics Anonymous.

The purpose of maintaining expectations at home is to add structure to your parenting skills, to promote family cohesiveness and to make it increasingly difficult for your child to use drugs. As we list the fundamental expectations that lend themselves to this process we strongly encourage you to keep it simple if you are adding some of your own expectations. A "laundry list" of household expectations will only be perceived by the adolescent as overwhelming.

Home:

1) *Follow the curfew guidelines.*

Your child may have begun to stay out later as his drug use progressed. Many of the clients with whom we work tell us they either never had a clear curfew or they would override it by sneaking out at night.

It is not conducive to the intervention process to allow your child to stay out late at night with his friends while you are expecting him to stop using drugs. Your child is not just giving up drugs. He is giving up his friends, hobbies, social support group and a large part of his identity; in short, his membership in the "drug culture." While staying out late with his friends from the drug culture he will be tempted, encouraged and pressured to use. Even if they do not directly ask him to smoke marijuana with them, just his watching others using in front of him will pressure him to use. If he does use, the drug culture will help him try to beat the urine analysis tests and con you. It is not prudent to your child's recovery for her to be out late with her friends. Consider the laws regarding curfew in your city for your own curfew guideline. You might want to let your child stay out an hour later on the weekends than on weeknights. Whatever the curfew guideline is, make sure that it is very clear.

2) *Complete chores by a specified time.*

If chores have never been an expectation for your child, then now is not the time to get your child to start doing chores. However, if doing chores has been an expectation, then you will want to list them on the *Setting Limits Contract.* Simply let her know what time the chores are expected to be completed. If, at the appointed time they are not completed, then implement the consequence. Your child will learn not to be dependent on your lecturing in order to complete her chores.

3) *Participate in family activities.*

When your child started to use drugs she might have begun to pull away from family activities. By structuring and encouraging family activities you are providing oppor-tunities for your child to find value in his family. Planning outdoor or other activities will further bring the family closer and make it increasingly difficult for your child to use drugs.

4) *Allow no drugs on the property.*

This expectation serves not only to protect your child from drug use but it also protects siblings from coming into contact with drugs. Keeping this expectation in mind, we encourage you to get rid of all the liquor in your home. Taking action such as this protects your child and lets her know you are making changes that encourage her recovery. Eliminating all alcohol from your home is a barometer of strong parental support.

This expectation also includes not allowing her friends to come over with drugs in their possession. Continued socialization with friends who use drugs is a setup for your child's relapse. Furthermore, these individuals pose a risk to you as a homeowner. In addition to the obvious legal implications of having certain drugs or people under the influence in your home, it is not uncommon for drug users themselves to steal from the parents of their friends.

As you probably realize, taking steps to ensure your child's recovery is an ongoing process that must be maintained at home as well as at school. Expectations regarding your child's experience at school will serve to hold him accountable for his academic participation. The following list of expectations provide a safety net so your child does not fall too far behind in school, whether he is in elementary school, middle school, high school, independent studies, junior college or a four-year college. This structure also makes it increasingly difficult for your child to use drugs.

School:

1) *Show up for all classes on time.*

Chances are your child arrived late to his classes as his drug use progressed. This may have led to your child not showing up for classes at all. This expectation helps him to get back into the role of being a responsible adolescent. Check your child's school attendance and academic progress weekly with the attendance office and his teachers.

2) *Complete all homework.*

You have probably noticed that your child's grades started to drop as a result of his drug use. Holding him accountable for completing homework will help him get back on track. Again, if your child is in elementary, junior high or high school, you can get weekly homework assignments from the teacher, or you can request that the teacher inform you if your child's homework is incomplete. Moreover, it will make it harder for him to spend time talking about or using drugs with his friends when he needs to be doing his schoolwork. If your child is in college it might be difficult to know if your child is completing his homework, however, you need to expect to see a copy of his semester report cards.

3) *Follow through with the rules of behavior at school.*

This holds your child accountable for adhering to the rules and norms of student behavior at his school. We encourage you to get a copy of the parent and student handbook from your child's school so you and your child both know what the expectations and consequences are for school. Do not assume that your adolescent will exercise common sense about these matters. Some children need clarification of certain topics. Some need specific, detailed discussion about what constitutes appropriate behavior. *You*, also, need to recognize and be confident that he or she has a good understanding of the expectations and consequences that are a part of campus life. If your child is in college, then it is important that you attend orientation so that you are familiar with the school's expectations and consequences.

4) *Maintain or improve your grade point average (GPA).*

You need to state clearly what grade point average (GPA) you expect your child to maintain. You want to establish a GPA goal that is reachable, not necessarily based on what you think his true potential is. If you make the expectation unrealistic it will only be a source of stress for the family and a setup for failure for your child. Consulting with your child's teachers and counselors will help you and your child in making this expectation appropriate and realistic.

Other:

Other important expectations to consider:

1) *Do not get into a car when the driver has used any drugs/alcohol.*

This expectation exists for the safety of your child. It also helps to inhibit your child's associations with people who choose to drink and drive. We have known many adolescents who have suffered physically, and some who have died, by choosing to ride in a vehicle that was driven by an intoxicated driver. Others have suffered great financial loss by having lawsuits brought against their families.

Every challenge in life is unique and has its own particular demands for coping or resolution. In the case of individuals trying to get drug free, the emphasis is on change: change in behaviors, thinking and attitudes. Parents must understand and recognize the motivation for change *specific* to the drug problem is pain. By pain, we are not talking about corporal punishment; we are not talking about punishment as a penalty. We are talking about consequences that must be implemented when behavioral objectives or expectations have not been met. Actions have consequences. This is one of life's realities. When you miss the bus, you're late for work. When you overeat, you have a stomachache. When you don't pay the phone bill, your line is disconnected. Such consequences entail inconvenience and added effort on the part of the person who initiated the original, corresponding action. While these examples cite relatively mild consequences, persons do incur more serious consequences. Consider the employee who is consistently late for and loses his job, or the individual who repeatedly fails to pay his rent and is subsequently evicted. These consequences are complicated and their effects extend to others. Consequences are painful then, if you think of them in terms of degrees of inconvenience and discomfort. For example, when your child is over eighteen, you may need to consider, as a consequence, your child moving out of your home.

Parents uncomfortable with the reality of logical consequences are apt to try to motivate their child with promises or rewards. One mistake many parents make when trying to get their child drug free is to "dangle a carrot" in front of their child. A parent might promise to buy her daughter a brand new car if she stops using drugs. We would love for this to be effective but our experience has been that it is not. Inhibiting drug behavior must be a closely monitored, constant process reinforced with immediate consequences for veering from the path of sobriety and recovery. We recognize that you might not feel comfortable with implementing consequences but it is absolutely necessary to help your child change.

While each child is unique, there are some common motivators among teenagers. It is likely that restriction of activities or suspending privileges will serve as an incentive to your child. We all know what it feels like to be disappointed and that feeling of frustration can be used in a positive way. The following is a list of popular adolescent attractions, some of which you might recognize as those that your child enjoys. These include skating, roller blading, snow skiing, snow boarding, water skiing, bike riding, talking on the phone, watching television, listening to music, playing video games, playing on the computer, socializing with friends, going to dances, receiving an allowance, having a work permit and driving a car. Temporarily depriving an adolescent of a beloved pastime can be a tool used to recapture her health and well-being. We strongly encourage you to embrace the process of recovery for your child and yourself. It is the necessary challenge.

Chapter 6

Your Child in Recovery

Recovering from a drug problem has unique characteristics. It is different from someone recovering from the flu or a broken bone. In each instance, we expect the restoration of one's health. In the case of the flu, there are many markers by which we can measure a person's recovery. A ninety-eight-degree body temperature, the absence of coughing, freedom from aches and pains and a good appetite collectively indicate a return to a healthy physical condition. The healing of a broken bone can be evaluated by an x-ray. An individual recovering from a drug problem must not only secure a return to physical well-being, but must also pursue methods to recapture or acquire emotional and *even* spiritual well-being for total restoration. This particular recovery process is unique because the damage caused by a drug problem is not limited to the user. It may be true that a parent having stayed up all night with a sick child will suffer the effects of fatigue or irritability the following day. Alternatively, a family dealing with a member's devastating chronic or terminal illness will experience worry, fatigue and most probably, grief. Now consider the relationship between parents and their child in the context of that child's drug use in order to understand the distinction between this type of recovery and recovery from other illnesses. Substance abuse compromises the emotional health of all family members. This happens in part because individual roles and responsibilities within the family system become enmeshed. In other words, some family members will make extraordinary efforts to compensate for those members unable or unwilling to perform their duties. For instance, if a parent recognizes the child is failing in school, he or she may do the child's homework for her. The mechanisms of denial and enabling stave off the fear people feel when they sense that their family isn't doing well. People want to keep their family afloat despite its dysfunction, and will take dramatic steps to insure that the *appearance* of a healthy family remains intact. Such efforts distort a balance in the family dynamics. The degree to which this has occurred can only be interpreted by individuals closely connected to the person with the drug problem, and by those family members actively participating within the family system. Furthermore, a drug problem undercuts honesty, trust, empathy and good judgment, the elements a family needs to operate smoothly. Recovering from a drug problem requires the rebuilding of relationships. Breaches of trust must be repaired. The uniqueness of this process is that it escapes a notable time frame and significant segments of the process are not observable to outsiders.

You have probably heard the phrase, "working a program of recovery." This refers to the subsequent ongoing, systematic efforts made towards the resumption of one's good health. When a child stops using drugs or alcohol, we refer to that action as abstinence. The behavioral and emotional changes that are incumbent on the newly abstinent adolescent would frighten the most courageous individuals. Though the changes occur over time, the work to bring about those changes must begin immediately. Dedication and commitment by the recovering person and her support network make the process effective. This work reflects a composition of strategies including counseling, nutrition education and recovery work. Parents must work together and in cooperation with the child's counselor and they must uphold their responsibilities for drug testing their child, exercising the *Setting Limits Contract* and attending *Alanon, Naranon* or *ToughLove®* meetings.

Seeking counseling for a drug problem is a healthy first step to recovery. A common concern heard from parents when they first contact our office is that their son or daughter does not *want* to go to counseling. It is a long-perpetuated myth that if a child does not want to go to counseling, then he or she is not ready to stop using drugs. This is not true. Kids who are using are not supposed to want to quit. In the beginning you can expect that your child will resist going to counseling. Your first task, by virtue of the contract, is to make him responsible for attending counseling sessions. It is natural and understandable that your son may be defensive and angry while you are driving him to his counselor's office. If your child is unwilling to go, do not cancel the appointment! Use this first session to discuss the ways in which you can hold him accountable for his refusal to go. A counselor who understands adolescence and adolescent drug use will likely be able to help your son to begin counseling and to start talking about his experience with drugs. We specifically recommend that you seek a counselor who is a specialist in substance abuse issues. It is usually the case that families treated by counselors who are *not* educated in drug problems spend much time, energy and money needlessly. It is imperative to immediately identify a drug problem because it influences all aspects of an individual's well being. An undiagnosed drug problem will compromise attempts to treat other emotional or mental health problems.

When counseling begins, the focus is on the child and parents sometimes feel like spectators to the process. It is beneficial for parents to recognize some pertinent aspects that accompany the process. It is important to note that the counselor-client relationship is one that depends on the elements of trust and confidentiality and takes time to develop. An effective counselor is able to extend to his or her client courtesy and respect. He or she acknowledges the client's value as a human being and listens to the client without judgment or criticism. As their relationship becomes established, it is the counselor's intent to help break the child's barrier of denial. Initially, clients are asked how their drug use caused problems for them. Typical responses to this inquiry are that it hasn't been a problem or that just having to come to counseling is a problem. As the counselor helps the client to recognize the negative consequences of his use and as the adolescent realizes the truth of his behavior, the mechanism of denial begins to disintegrate. Then responses to the counselor's original question are more apt to sound like the following: "Well, I don't talk with my family. They don't trust me and I'm not really interested in them." "I'm not applying myself in school like I have in the past." "I don't like being around non-drug-using friends." "I find that I spend most of my money on drugs." "All of the problems I have had with the law are related to my drug use." "Girlfriends I have had expressed concern about my drug use." "I don't like myself these days because I have really compromised my values. Yet, I still want to use drugs." These last statements reflect the child's honesty and indicate that he is preparing to come to terms with the reality of his situation.

In counseling, your child will be encouraged to describe an accurate history of her chemical use. The negative consequences of her use will be carefully explored. The object of this process is for the child to realize the truth about her drug use. She will then be free to establish new goals and healthy patterns of behavior. As adolescents gain trust in their counselor, many become willing to speak with greater frankness and detail about the facts of their drug use. Sometimes clients are instructed to maintain a journal to record their thoughts and feelings. In our own practice and only in our presence , we encourage our clients to share the accurate account of their drug use with their parents. Early in the intervention process both the adolescent and family are vulnerable and it is to everyone's advantage to have the expertise and guidance of the counselor. Additionally, this particular setting requires a climate of respect and one in which all participants withhold judgment toward the child. It is imperative that parents refrain from punishing their child for any incident she reveals that occurred in the past. The counselor's presence is likely to be enough to ensure this climate of respect. This encounter allows a client and his or her family to listen *carefully* to each other. Perhaps proper listening skills were absent in recent family conversations. Maybe they never existed. Listening to one another with true concern is a necessary skill for families that desire healthy communication. We seek this type of communication for interpersonal relationships, especially family relationships. A client listing the details of her drug use may be thought to be solely demonstrating an *intellectual* exercise. When this same adolescent has the courage to share the details of her drug involvement with the people she loves, she can begin to understand the *emotional* impact she has had on others as they each communicate to her the ways in which her drug use has affected them.

Listening is the way to validate the person to whom you are listening. It is the critical path to understanding others. For example, think about a mother who yells at her daughter for a broken curfew. The child hears anger and ranting and, naturally, a child wants to block that out. If this mother could calmly express her love for her daughter by stating how frightened she was for her safety, she would be more apt to maintain the lines of communication and have the opportunity to explore the reasons for her daughter's behavior. That is not to say that her daughter should escape a consequence for breaking her curfew. However, this is a separate matter. The greater issue is that their relationship remains intact and that communication is preserved. This is largely accomplished through careful listening. Furthermore, when people are free to state their true feelings, there will be greater understanding available to enhance a relationship. Meeting with your child and her counselor will be an opportunity to learn to communicate more effectively, reestablish openness and honesty in your relationship with your child and will serve to further the recovery process. *You want* to trust your child just as *you want* your child to trust you. This step is *your* chance to act on that desire. If you want a meaningful relationship with your child starting now, it is up to you to be mindful of the seriousness of this step.

After your child has maintained a period of abstinence, his counselor can help him deal with emotions and feelings he was either not aware of or was unable to express during his drug use. With chemical use, individuals are unable to identify the depth, range or the variety of feelings they experience. For many adolescents the most commonly described feelings are boredom or anger. We might ask a client how he felt when his grandmother died. He might state apathetically that he has no feelings about her death or that it was probably best for her. If we inquire about how he felt after breaking up with his girlfriend he may simply state that he was angry while his other emotions such as hurt, shame and sadness remain suppressed or left unrecognized.

People in the early stages of chemical abstinence often describe this period as an "emotional roller coaster." To some parents, it appears that their child is still on drugs. Typically, this is a time characterized by extreme mood shifts and we know it can be very trying for parents. Your child is abstinent and no longer medicating his feelings with drugs. That is everyone's wish. However, you must understand the difficulty that he may experience as he confronts his emotions directly and attempts to find new ways in which to cope. It is also everyone's wish that he will develop positive changes in his attitude, emotional expression, behavior and interpersonal relationships. It is understandable that loved ones want these changes to occur quickly even though they know it requires time and patience. It can also be a confusing time. Although your son may be sad, he may act as if he is mad. Early recovery is an important time for your child to learn to identify and express his newly felt emotions. Initially, the adolescent will express himself in vague terms such as, "I feel weird," or "I feel bad." It is the counselor's job to help your child find words that reflect these feelings specifically and accurately. Together they will explore fear, happiness, boredom, pain, sadness, joy, peacefulness, anxiety, depression, agitation, guilt and shame.

As your child begins to identify his emotions, he will realize the extent to which his feelings were numbed with drugs. He will be able to see the necessity of learning effective coping skills and he will learn how to express his emotions appropriately. Formerly, he may have been verbally abusive or used threatening, aggressive behavior to achieve his goals. In recovery, his counselor will help him to find acceptable ways to communicate. In the same way that an athlete trains for a competitive event, your child will need time and opportunities to build his newly acquired skills. He *will* get stronger over time. Parents are encouraged to maintain reasonable expectations and cautioned not to minimize the strides, however small, that their child is making. If you are unclear about any aspect of the counseling process, or have questions regarding expectations for your child or questions about your responsibilities in recovery, feel free to ask those questions and convey your concerns to your child's counselor. Your participation and interest can enrich and accelerate the process of recovery.

Counseling also provides an opportunity for your child to examine any deeper, unresolved emotional conflicts. An astute counselor will be able to identify other serious medical issues such as bipolar disease, attention-deficit disorder or depression. It may be that your child will need further care from another appropriate source such as a psychiatrist, psychologist or other specialized health-care provider.

With his counselor your child may need to discuss how he has been affected by his parents' divorce, the death of a loved one, or how he has been shunned by his social group. This process allows the child to recapture his emotional self and health. When an individual is using drugs, emotional maturity is arrested. The focus of that person's life has been his relationship with chemicals. In recovery, individuals are playing "catch up." Time, patience, diligence and consistency are required for your child's growth.

Many chemical dependency counselors recognize drug addiction as a physical, emotional and spiritual illness. Frequently, these practitioners and twelve-step programs of recovery focus on the emotional and spiritual aspects of the illness and overlook the physical link. For example, a person in a program of recovery, which includes counseling and twelve-step work through *Alcoholics Anonymous* or *Narcotics Anonymous,* may exhibit symptoms such as irritability, depression, aggressiveness, insomnia, fatigue, restlessness, confusion, nervousness or a desire to drink. She may be told by her counselor or members of the twelve-step program that she is in a "dry drunk," and she needs to work harder on her recovery. The term "dry drunk" has been used to describe a person who is not using drugs but is still acting as if she were. We know from the research of Emanuel Cheraskin, M.D., as cited in Joan Mathews Larson's book, *Seven Weeks to Sobriety,* that the behaviors an individual experiences in a "dry-drunk" mimic the symptoms of hypoglycemia: irritability, depression, aggressiveness, insomnia, fatigue, restlessness, confusion, nervousness and a desire to drink. According to Cheraskin, seventy five to ninety percent of all alcoholics have hypoglycemia, a condition that is characterized by abnormally low blood sugar.[1] It is important that a physician who has an interest in chemical dependency assess the state of your child's health. A nutritionist may need to advise your child on dietary treatment and education.

Currently, your child may be deficient in vitamins, minerals and amino acids as a result of her drug use. Inadequate diet and genetic predispositions can create these deficiencies too. *Seven Weeks to Sobriety* illustrates a program of nutrition and provides a thorough discussion of what happens to the body during the early weeks of recovery. *The Diet Cure*, by Julia Ross explores health issues common to people with addictions.[2] Proper nutrition is essential to meeting the needs of the body and cannot be discounted at the time your child stops using drugs. A nutrition evaluation is necessary to allow for continued progress in recovery. Counseling without acknowledging the biological needs of someone recovering from a drug problem can undermine the emotional and spiritual recovery work.

Experts in the field of chemical dependency recovery know that those individuals who incorporate a spiritual component to their program are apt to have the greatest chance for success. They tend to experience a more balanced and fulfilling program. It is not within the scope of this book to define this part of recovery. Spirituality is strictly individual and personal. However, compassion and respect for oneself and others are two components inherent in most spiritual traditions and are critical to recovery as well. One of the places people learn to define what spirituality means to them is at a twelve-step meeting. The "twelve steps" are the principles and practices that guide a chemically dependent individual in the process of recovery. You may obtain a copy of *Alcoholics Anonymous*[3/] (also known as the "Big Book") at any *A.A.* meeting or a *Narcotics Anonymous* text at any *Naranon* meeting. It will explain the program and the steps in detail. These meetings also foster self-awareness and development of healthy relationships with others. They allow your child the opportunity to bond with others by recognizing the similarities they share not only with their drug use but also with their life experiences.

We encourage your child to look for the similarities that he shares with people at the meetings rather than dwelling on their differences. Why? Focusing on differences he observes between himself and others will keep him on the outskirts of recovery and will contribute to his denial that he has a drug or alcohol problem. He must become a part of the process itself if there is to be a restoration of health and well-being. He might tell you that many people who attend the meetings are older than he is. He may remark that they used different drugs than he did or that they used needles while he did not. We want to remind him that there are important similarities among members, two of which include drug tolerance and persistent preoccupation with drug use. They may also share financial, legal or self-esteem problems or they may have similar problems at school, home or on the job.

It is important for your child to find a twelve-step meeting where he feels comfortable. He needs to find a meeting where he feels safe to share his experience with drugs and reflect on how he was affected. Good meetings for adolescents trying to stay drug-free are often meetings that include a mix of adults and adolescents. Some adolescent meetings consist of youth who do not take their recovery seriously because the courts, probation officers or counselors made their attendance mandatory. A mix of adults and adolescents allows for the group's stability and can preserve the goals and traditions that are important to recovery. Moreover, adults with greater maturity can model recovery and healthy behaviors. They can also be a source of sponsorship.

Sponsorship is an important element for anyone participating in a twelve-step program. Your child's sponsor will be an integral part in your child's recovery as he facilitates the twelve-step work. He will work with your son to examine your child's powerlessness over drugs. He will help your adolescent to embark on a spiritual quest, one that will help to sustain your child's sobriety. Additionally, he will help your child take an honest look at his personal shortcomings or character defects and make amends to the people he has harmed.

A sponsor is someone who has a significant amount of "clean time," or abstinence and is working the twelve steps. He is a person who can mentor your child throughout his recovery and help him work the twelve steps. Your child's sponsor must be the same sex as your child because this allows for healthy modeling. Men must have the opportunity to work on men's recovery issues and women to work on their own recovery issues. A sponsor should have at least three years of sobriety. He should have a good knowledge of the steps, the pains and joys of recovery and the overall process of the program.

In his twelve-step group, your son will learn to take care of himself and then to extend that sense of caring to others. It is not natural for a person who has been hiding from his own feelings by using drugs to feel comfortable sharing heartfelt matters with others in a group, but it is an imperative part of the recovery process. By attending meetings your child will learn about intimacy. Many of the adolescents with whom we work equate intimacy with sex. They do not recognize that intimacy entails an exchange in which people reveal themselves both emotionally and intellectually. Intimacy involves risk-taking. Individuals need to be able to disclose matters of importance, especially those that will influence their recovery, in a safe environment and one that honors respect and confidentiality. When we verbalize our deepest thoughts and feelings, we run the risk of becoming vulnerable to the scrutiny of others. For some, this can be both frightening and overwhelming.

In a twelve-step environment, the members are expected to adhere to the elements of compassion and respect creating a desirable climate in which parties are free to share their questions, insights and support for one another. **Confidentiality and anonymity are paramount components to twelve-step programs.** Participants use their first names only. There is no pressure to disclose one's personal experience, but this usually occurs naturally as people recognize the effectiveness of the program. In the beginning, you might want to attend a few meetings with your child until she is comfortable on her own. The settings for the meetings vary and are not at all formal. Meetings are often held in a hospital basement, church meeting hall, or in a vacant room above a shopping center. Attire is definitely come as you are! Usually a "secretary," (no one takes notes) conducts the meeting and keeps an orderly flow of conversation. While there is plenty of talking, you are always free to sit quietly and say nothing.

Adolescents benefit from their participation in recovery as they begin to recognize positive changes in themselves. They feel a sense of empowerment as they exercise self-discipline to follow a program of recovery and they demonstrate a willingness to learn new behaviors and adopt attitudes that augment their good health. They begin to reestablish trust with themselves and others and they learn to set reasonable goals and to find new passions to enjoy. Formerly, your child may have exhibited what is termed "junkie pride." She may have bragged wildly about how she was able to smoke more marijuana than her peers. Now she might express "recovery pride" because it feels good to be clean and sober. When adolescents have pride in their sobriety date, the date of their first day of abstinence, they are taking full responsibility for their behavior. This is an excellent indicator that they are truly in recovery.

Another area of concern in recovery is that of relapse. Recovery constitutes a major life change. Rarely do adolescents start treatment, become abstinent and begin working on recovery without relapsing. Understandably, there will be feelings of disappointment, sadness and concern if your child relapses. Many parents erroneously expect their child will achieve perfection while in counseling and attending twelve-step meetings. Remember that recovery is a process and is subject to continual intervention and the discovery of a child's relapse is an opportunity for parents to intervene. Does relapse mean that an individual in recovery is back to the beginning? No! Only one's sobriety date has changed. It's possible that the recovering individual has made several significant life-style changes and that progress remains in tact. Changes may include better grades in school, new hobbies or a more respectful attitude toward parents.

Many factors contribute to relapse, including loneliness and boredom. Other conditions that precipitate relapse may be the individual's biological makeup, physical or social cravings, internal or environmental stimuli and peer pressure. In addition to reading about the biology of addiction, we recommend that you read, *Adolescent Relapse Warning Signs,* an excellent booklet by Tammy L. Bell. This publication lists thirty-nine behavioral relapse warning signs.[4]/

While it is everyone's hope that relapse does not happen, it is essential to understand what can trigger a relapse. When we use the word "trigger" we are specifically referring to those people, places and things that were once associated with your child's experience of intoxication. For example, if your daughter always got intoxicated behind the movie theater, then going behind the movie theater while being abstinent from drugs would elicit memories of being intoxicated. These memories reinforce the desire to use. When your child is exposed to her "triggers," she will start to think about her drug use and this, in itself, may be enough to cause her to relapse. After identifying her "triggers," she will recognize the importance of avoiding exposure to them. In counseling and her twelve-step program she will learn how to handle associated memories as they occur and will learn to accept her limitations as a necessary part of her recovery.

Gradually, your child will see that she needs to move away from the drug culture. Remember, she received many benefits from participating in the drug culture. She had friends, acceptance, support and approval. She had a social life and an identity. These are the things that adolescents hope for and work hard to attain. It's easy to see that having to give all these things up, especially all at once, could be overwhelming for an adolescent. It can prove to be a difficult struggle. Even though she cannot use drugs, she still craves the people, places and things associated with the past. The reality is that these social "cravings" present a juncture for the child that will result in the child finding a new social group or relapsing.

To understand this, imagine that you have a job in a bakery. While at work you have the opportunity to watch customers smile when they bite into the freshly baked chocolate chip cookies. You observe and hear people sharing a delightful experience as they taste the baked goods and you are very much a beneficiary of that joy. Then, during a visit with your physician, you are diagnosed with diabetes. The consumption of a diet high in carbohydrates, sugar and fats would be detrimental to your health. You would be forced to make dramatic changes in your eating habits. For this reason, a bakery would probably not be a favorable place to work.

Think about the many activities and people with which your child was associated. Consider your own personal and social life. Recovery is about replacing old, unhealthy behaviors with new and productive behaviors. It's about developing friendships based on mutual interests and respect. New passions must be found that can satisfy your child's zest for living. Your child is responsible for his own recovery. You cannot do it for him. **This is tough stuff.** It is important to implement ongoing support for you child including counseling, medical care and twelve-step groups. Your responsibility is to hold him accountable. Your child needs *your* help. He needs your presence, your tenderness, your strength and your support.

Chapter 7

Your Family in Recovery

The greatest opportunity for a child's recovery from a drug problem lies within the context of the child's own family. Earlier, we stated the three prime areas of focus that pertain to child and adolescent recovery as counseling, nutrition education and twelve-step meetings for the chemically dependent individual. We also discussed the unique aspect of this specific kind of recovery as one in which all family members are affected. Ultimately, the adolescent will choose whether or not he will use drugs. Recovery is not guaranteed. However, if he or she is to have the optimal chance for recovery, the individual's family must provide the proper environment and support. For all families, this means undergoing change. Some families will need to make dramatic changes. Part of changing is being open to the advice of others and being willing to look within yourself to examine the motives for your behavior.

In a family parents are viewed as leaders, main financial providers and those who have the power to set a positive example during the process of recovery. It may be the case, however, that parents themselves are struggling with their own addictions and unhealthy parenting behaviors. Clearly, such unresolved problems complicate and sabotage the adolescent's chance for recovery. **Recovery for yourself or spouse is key to your child's recovery.** If you or your partner is experiencing problems with alcohol or drugs, your child's chances for recovery are greatly diminished.   Recovery from addiction and unhealthy parenting behavior *is* possible, however. Family members need to work individually and simultaneously to maintain the common goal of recovery.

Parents must deal directly with areas in need of personal repair, which may include addiction problems, unhealthy parenting behaviors, gaining insight to the family in which they were raised and divorce. We will comment briefly on each issue and provide you with questions and observations to heighten your awareness about the impact these problems have on the family, and, how they undermine your child's efforts to recover from his own drug problem.

Addictions can include alcoholism or drug dependence, sex addiction, overeating or overspending. It might even be the case that, although *you* are certain that you do not have a problem, the reality is that you do. If you use any illegal drugs yourself, you have a drug problem. If you or your spouse use prescription medications in higher doses than prescribed or use prescriptions that are not your own, you have a drug problem. It might be more difficult to recognize your own alcohol problem. Has anyone close to you such as your spouse, ex-spouse or friend ever commented that you drink too much? At times, do you drink frequently or drink more than you intend to? If you are not certain seek a professional evaluation of your own use. Ask you child's counselor for a referral.

Even if you or your spouse is not chemically dependent, it is important during this time in your child's recovery, for you to remove all alcohol from your home.

Remember, being in an environment where drugs are being used is a risk factor for relapse. Remove any prescriptions and over-the-counter medications that contain intoxicating ingredients. (Ask the counselor or a pharmacist which substances those might include.) In doing so you will eliminate some temptation for your child and you will be sending him the message that you are dedicated to his recovery. These actions demonstrate healthy parenting and positive role modeling. If the thought of disposing of your alcohol makes you feel uncomfortable, this is an indication that you may have a problem with alcohol. All cessation of addiction problems begins with the recognition and admission of the problem. It is important to recognize that it is probably your own fears keeping you from changing and seeking help. If you sense that you have a problem, follow the same path of recovery as recommended for your child: seek counseling, tend to your physical health and attend the appropriate twelve-step meetings. There is a twelve-step meeting designed for each type of addiction. It is our hope that as you seek help you will develop understanding so that you will not feel angry and resentful for having to quit your own use. Furthermore, the purpose of this discussion is *not* for you to diagnose another person, but to initiate self-examination. If you *do* recognize your spouse has a problem, your role in his recovery is to seek your own recovery by attending *Alanon* meetings. Getting help for yourself will facilitate your ability to intervene in your spouse's addiction.

We will preface our discussion of unhealthy parenting by restating the two most destructive behaviors that serve to undermine your child's recovery; they are denial and enabling. These behaviors allow your child to stay active in his drug use. Briefly, they keep your child from realizing the negative consequences of his drug use and they keep him from developing a sense of responsibility and self-discipline. Please refer to the fourth chapter of this book to see how denial and enabling work to keep your child from progressing in recovery and to understand the necessity for relinquishing their use. Your behavior need not be dictated by your child's behavior. Only when you stop denying that your child has a problem with drugs and stop enabling him, will *you* begin to develop peace within yourself, even if the circumstances of your child's life do not change.

In an effort to understand your own parenting style, it is helpful to review the behaviors that originated in the family in which you grew up. Of course, many of you were the recipients of sound parenting. Some of you though, emerged from a family setting which included a mix of both constructive and destructive parenting behaviors. Some behaviors will be noted as unmistakably injurious while a counselor's help may be needed to help you to recognize other, more subtle unhealthy actions. Part of the process of seeking help is accepting that you are not perfect. You have made mistakes. We all have. Both you and your child can heal from those mistakes. The healing comes from identifying the unhealthy behaviors and then adopting effective behaviors to replace them. At first, it might be helpful to sit down and make a list of the things you are doing that you know in your heart, are not what you should be doing. Writing things down can facilitate the recognition that there is a problem. Some behaviors that you know are inappropriate include physical or verbal abuse and threats. Sarcasm, too, can compromise healthy communication. You might feel sad or guilty admitting this type of conduct. Even though these emotions might be difficult to feel, view them as important elements for change.

To augment an understanding of your personal history, a key question to ask yourself is whether there was a history of chemical dependency in your family. If there was, we recommend three excellent books on this subject: *It Will Never Happen To Me*, by Claudia Black,[1] *Breaking the Cycle of Addiction*, by Patricia O'Gorman and Philip Oliver-Diaz[2] and *Adult Children of Alcoholics*, by Janet Geringer Woititz, Ed.D.[3] As noted in *It Will Never Happen To Me* by Claudia Black, there are several commonalities among families with addiction or substance abuse problems. Four points characterize such families:

1) There is a need for rigid perfectionism and control.

2) It is not okay to talk about problems within the family.

3) It is not okay to trust people because promises are frequently broken.

4) It is not okay to express your feelings or you simply do not know how. [4]

Your past experiences remain a part of you and affects you today. A large part of human behavior is learned through the processes of observation and *modeling*. Children imitate the behaviors that their parents demonstrate. Those behaviors, constructive or not, can be carried into adulthood. Certainly, we are not responsible for the behaviors exhibited by people in our family of origin. However, we *are* responsible for our own recovery, and this includes recovery from unhealthy parenting. You may ask what typifies unhealthy behavior. Instead, let's begin by stating three fundamental needs a family must provide its members to sustain healthy functioning. According to J. Woititz, parents and children, *all* family members, must be able to express and have their feelings validated.[5] Adults and children must live together in an environment that is consistent and within acceptable parameters of behavior.

If you emerged from a family in which these factors were lacking, it is unlikely that you would know how to provide them for your own spouse and children. Perhaps you have had some awareness that your own parents conducted their relationships with limited skills. Maybe you readily identified abusive behavior. Having been treated unjustly is not immunity against unhealthy parenting behavior. Sometimes people repeat the same negative behaviors towards their children as their own parents used with them even though they promised themselves that that would never happen. For instance, if it was generally the case that your father yelled or called you names while trying to get you to accomplish a task or get better grades, you may have insisted you would never treat your own child similarly. As an adult, however, you may be inclined to act the very same way, especially under stressful conditions.

Healthy parenting involves respect, both for oneself and for those with whom one is dealing. Children need boundaries in order to feel safe and it is up to their parents to create a balanced environment that includes reasonable behavioral expectations and open, clear and regular communication. Two publications that we strongly recommend are *Positive Discipline* and *Positive Discipline for Teenagers*, both by Jane Nelsen, Ed.D.[6 & 7] Additionally, we remind you to attend, *ToughLove®*, twelve-step meetings or both. Most communities offer parenting classes as well. You may be able to discontinue some destructive behaviors by recognizing them as harmful. **Becoming a more effective parent means being receptive to change, seeking new ways of relating to your child and being vigilant about not reverting to old patterns of behavior.**

Many families maintain two households due to divorce. Dealing with a child's drug problem requires that parents present a united front. Children are sensitive to the feelings and problems of their parents. It is naïve to think that the anger or resentment you feel can be hidden from your children. The inability to resolve problems experienced in a former marriage or in the process of divorce will only complicate the relationship with your child. You need to be on your guard to avoid taking your anger towards a former spouse out on your child. If, in your former marriage you tended to sulk and isolate yourself when your feelings were hurt, you might do the same in your relationship with your children. Furthermore, efforts to compensate for the painful effects of divorce, such as indulging your child or making your child your confident or best friend are unhealthy.

No matter how long it has been since your divorce, you might still need to seek help toward recovery. Recovery is not just moving forward with your external life. It is often hard to accept the fact that your hopes and dreams of what life was supposed to be have changed. As with other losses, it is normal to grieve while trying to accept your new life. Acceptance begins by talking with others about your situation and feelings. Help can come from a professional counselor or from a divorce recovery group at a local church or community center.

Families working toward recovery are to be admired. Theirs is a weighty task. It is encouraging, however, to realize the vast amount of support that is available and to know that each person can secure his or her own return to a peaceful life.

Chapter 8

Encouragement

It has been our intention to familiarize you thoroughly with the nature of the drug problem. The availability of drugs and the prevalence of adolescent drug problems across our nation is strong evidence that necessitates the same attention as the attention given to all problems that affect the welfare of our youth. As you have probably realized, the problem itself can present a broad range of complexities. The most important thing to recognize, however, is that a drug problem does not cure itself. It does not go away without implementing particular actions. Currently, there is a prominent advertising campaign, which states that, "Action is the anti-drug." It's true! Parents concerned about the health and well-being of their children are in an optimal position to initiate such actions. To some degree, parents still maintain the legal and economic advantage that can facilitate a course of behavioral changes in children or young adults. Remember that it is not necessary to have your child's permission, cooperation or desire to stop using drugs in order for you to intercede in this behavior, and there are many resources you can enlist to support your efforts to resolve this problem. Some of the resources are of no monetary cost to you. When there is a fee involved, sometimes it will be based on what an individual family can afford. Do not be afraid to ask a counselor or physician about this.

There is a plan that parents can implement to attempt to get their child drug free. There are combinations of strategies that can be tailored to meet the needs of individuals and their families. There is a tool available, *The Setting Limits Contract,* which we know to be very effective in the management of an adolescent drug problem. Still, some parents hesitate to act.

It is interesting to consider the many types problems that we encounter in life. It is interesting, also, to consider why we are willing to tackle some problems and not others. A drug problem is a tough one. Often, it is not easy to recognize, admit to or give up. Many people have glommed onto the old perception that a resolution to a drug problem is insurmountable. That perception is outdated! People *can* do something about it. The problem is widespread and doesn't target a particular population. We are all susceptible to its ill effects. Therefore, it really makes sense to become informed about this issue and to learn about the techniques available to inhibit or arrest its progression.

Why then, do people hesitate to seek help? We mentioned in Chapter 1 that fear is a prominent deterrent to seeking help and making the changes necessary to resolving a drug problem. Additionally, attacking this particular problem requires effort to define exactly what the problem is and who has been affected. A drug problem is complex and needs to be broken into manageable parts. A professional may be helpful in this regard. In general, problem solving requires making decisions. Resolving a drug problem requires many decisions, both big and small. However, they don't all have to be made at once. Problem solving is a skill. **People can learn to be problem solvers.** As they practice defining a problem, breaking it into manageable parts and making necessary decisions, they will become more adept with each subsequent experience.

If you think there is a drug problem at hand, we encourage you to seek a resolution. You've already begun the process by reading this book. Don't stop! Continue your search. Use the library and the internet to learn about drugs. Find a counselor who specializes in adolescents and drug issues for a professional evaluation. Ask your network of friends; a school counselor; or local church for referrals. Check local and neighborhood newspapers for dates and times of twelve-step meetings. Twelve-step programs are also listed in the telephone book.

As you pursue a resolution to this problem, you will undoubtedly meet some knowledgeable and caring people. Let them help. You do not have to be alone in this experience. Nor should you be. Working on a difficult problem requires focus, concentration and support. It also requires intermittent respite from the hard work. Sometimes taking a break will allow you to return to the work with a new perspective. Perhaps, there will be times that you will simply have to recommit to working on the problem. That's okay. The parents and guardians of our clients who have the greatest success are those who persevere. They are open to new information and question any aspect of the recovery process that seems confusing. They accept setbacks but maintain their commitment to conflict resolution. They call on their child's counselor to help them accurately interpret the elements of the problem and to understand the accompanying emotions. We encourage you to do the same.

Yes, a drug problem is a tough one. However, as counselors we are so grateful to have had the opportunity to observe families throughout the healing process. We have watched clients and parents reconcile by learning to communicate with each other. We have witnessed incredible strength in our clients as they learn to utilize their newfound understanding of their problem. We have seen them act independently and with maturity. The greatest satisfaction of all, however, has been to hear an individual express a genuine appreciation for the unique person he or she is. This is the best possible outcome and we want this for your child and your family.

Notes

Chapter 1

1. Inaba, Darryl S., and William E. Cohen. <u>Uppers, Downers, All Arounder: Physical and Mental Effects of Psychoactive Drugs</u>. 5th ed. Ashland (OR): CNS Publications, 2004, pp 57-58.

2. ---. pp. 62-63.

3. ---. p. 87.

Chapter 4

1. Beattie, Melody. <u>Codependent No More: How to Stop Controlling Others and Start Caring for Yourself</u>. Center City (MN): Hazelden, 1987, p. 36.

Chapter 5

1. "Comparative Causes of Annual Deaths in the United States" Center for Disease Control and Prevention, Department of Health and Human Services. <<u>http://www.cdc.gov/tobacco/research_data/</u> health_consequences/mortali.htm> and search for "andths".

2. Stuyt, Elizabeth B. "Nicotine Might Play a Role in Substance Abuse." <u>The American Journal of Addictions</u>. 6 (1997), pp. 159-167.

3. Hurt, Richard, et al. "Mortality Following Inpatient Addictions Treatment: Role of Tobacco Use in a Community-based Cohort." <u>JAMA</u> 275 (1996), pp. 1097-1103.

Chapter 6

1. Larson, Joan M. <u>Seven Weeks to Sobriety: The Proven Program to Fight Alcoholism through Nutrition</u>. New York: Fawcett Columbine, 1992, p. 117.

2. Ross, Julia. <u>The Diet Cure</u>. New York: Penguin, 1999.

3. Alcoholics Anonymous World Services, <u>Alcoholics Anonymous</u>, New York: Alcoholics Anonymous World Services, Inc., revised 2001.

4. Bell, Tammy L. <u>Adolescent Relapse Warning Signs</u>. Independence (MO): Herald House/Independence Press, 1989.

Chapter 7

1. Black, Claudia. <u>It Will Never Happen to Me!</u>. Denver: M.A.C., 1981.

2. O'Gorman, Patricia, and Philip Oliver-Diaz. <u>Breaking the Cycle of Addiction: For Adult Children of Alcoholics</u>. Deerfield Beach (FL): Health Communications, Inc., (1987).

3. Woititz, Janet G. <u>Adult Children of Alcoholics</u>. Exp. ed. Deerfield Beach (FL): Health Communications, Inc., (1990).

4. Black, Claudia. <u>It Will Never Happen to Me!</u>. Denver: M.A.C., 1981, pp. 4, 33, 39, 46.

5. Woititz, Janet G. <u>Adult Children of Alcoholics</u>. Exp. ed. Deerfield Beach (FL): Health Communications, Inc., (1990), pp. 84, 90, 100.

6. Nelsen, Jane, Ed.D. <u>Positive Discipline</u>. New York: Ballentine Books (1996).

7. ---. <u>Positive Discipline for Teenagers</u>. Prima Publications (1994).